The Five Spheres of Transformation
Katie T. Miller

Between us and goodness, the gods have placed the sweat of our brows. *Hesiod*

Table of Contents

Introduction..1

First Principles

The Power of the Universe...9
The Power of You..17
The Power of Others..23

Getting off the Ground

Home Base: Life in the Troposphere............................33
    Accept & Let Go Chapter Companion..................47

Sphere of Fear: Life in the Stratosphere.......................53
    Seek Inner Courage Chapter Companion 66

State of Being: Life in the Mesosphere.........................75
    Change your Habits Chapter Companion..............88

Experiencing your Greatest Transformation

Self Mastery: Life in the Thermosphere........................113
    Evoke your Highest Self Chapter Companion ……..125

Joy & Freedom: Life in the Exosphere.........................133
    Navigate your Life Chapter Companion…………....145

Bibliography..153

To my parents and my sister for planting the seed.
My husband and daughters, for putting up with a writer.
And for every woman who holds this book, this is for you.

She fell and she fell and she fell, over the edge of blackness

Introduction

My story as I knew it ended in the throes of grief. For over a year I stumbled through various stages of denial, isolation, anger, and bargaining; and it was there, in that painful and terrifying loneliness, as a denizen of the deep, that I came to know the first sphere of transformation. Lost in a seemingly bottomless chasm of beliefs -about myself, my life, and the people that I loved -I learned that the only way to escape my despair was to push my way through it, one layer at a time, or risk floating into darkness. There were no shortcuts or faking it this time; I had to lie utterly naked beside my truth. Eventually, I could see that it was not some mysterious abyss I was pushing my way through, but that it was my own consiousness expanding, one layer at a time, until I had finally come to know what it meant to feel a sense of peace in my life. Perhaps that's why you picked up this book. Maybe you're somewhere in the void, also wanting to be free from the pain -whatever that pain is for you. Perhaps someone you love has hurt you, or you're tired and don't feel like you know who you are anymore. Maybe you believe in your heart that you are capable of more, but you're afraid of failure or judgment, or you're simply curious and want to learn a new way to approach your daily life and routines. Whatever has brought you here, I honor your courage. Choosing this book means you are seeking a change in your life, which is often the most difficult part of the journey. It took several years for me to understand the five spheres of transformation, to somehow craft them into words that could provide a clear pathway for others, but I've spent a lifetime in the spheres, and so have you. If you take the time to sit with yourself and ponder what is in this book, you will learn how to consciously ascend through each layer of your own beliefs, your own fears, your own resilience, and your own self-mastery, while discovering a clear path for how to create a meaningful transformation in your life. This book is your invitation to take flight on a journey towards finding joy and freedom in *your* way and on *your* terms. All you need to do is begin.

This Book Explained

The first step towards any change only takes a little imagination. Oftentimes we feel ready for something new, but breaking down *how* a transformation can happen is why I wrote this book. The image below serves as a simple but powerful visual tool comparing five distinct stages of growth to the five layers of our atmosphere. Atmospheric layers are distinguished only by the changes in temperature that occur within them. Similarly, the layers of our mental and spiritual growth are characterized only by the changes in perception that occur within *us* as we evolve. The atmosphere inside of us is a beautiful analogy that can be used to bring us from our lowest state of constant struggle into our highest state of joy and freedom.

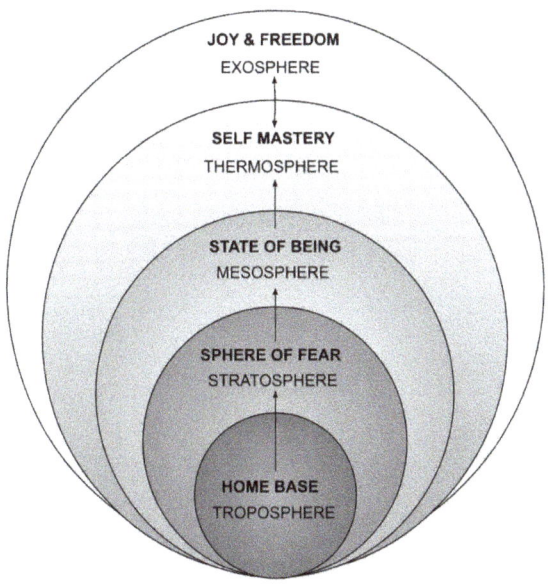

This book is divided into three parts. Part one, *First Principles,* sets the tone as it outlines the foundational concepts of *The Five Spheres of Transformation*; ideas about the universe, interconnectedness, and meaning; about our power, energy, and intelligence; and the power of others through the lens of pain, forgiveness, and heart-consciousness. Each principle, *The Power of the Universe*, *The Power of You,* and the *Power of Others,* gently invites you into thinking about your spiritual beliefs, inner strength, and pain points. As you move into part two, *Getting Off The Ground*, the first three spheres of transformation are introduced: *Home Base*, *Sphere of Fear*, and *State of Being*. Just as in life, each sphere builds on the other. Through a mix of storytelling, anecdotes, and proposed action, this section of the book will sweep you into the subtleties of childhood and memory, leading you to explore how you first learned to interpret your circumstances and shape yourself over time. In part three, *Experiencing Your Greatest Transformation*, the fourth and fifth spheres of transformation are introduced. These final two spheres, *Self Mastery* and *Joy & freedom*, show how the never-ending pursuit of progress is our masterpiece of life. It is in this section of the book where, after being guided out of the default pattern of living that you've always known in your home base, you can begin to experience, with passion and purpose, the life that you want. Embedded throughout the book is the A.S.C.E.N.D Personal Journal, which has been divided into a series of chapter companions. The journal follows the five unique stages of growth and was designed to complement each sphere of transformation. It provides practical exercises and resources that can bring a more rooted and personalized context to your reading. The exercises are not meant to be completed all at once, rather it would be best if each exercise were completed in such a way that would leave you coming back to the book and deepening your understanding over time.

Generally speaking, one will naturally gravitate to the messages in this book, as well as the exercises, when it is called to them. Just as temperature changes inform what is possible in each layer of our atmosphere, our lives unfold very much the same way, with every challenge we must break through inside of ourselves taking us from one height to the next. As you work through these five spheres of transformation, my hope is that you will begin to feel lighter physically, mentally, and spiritually. This book is here as a guide, and the lessons found inside will take each individual a different measure of time to absorb. In fact, there is no point where Earth officially ends and outer space begins, and there is no place where you will someday arrive in taking this journey. This book does not promise a final endpoint or nirvana, but something better.

Part 1

First Principles

First Principles
The Power of the Universe

I once had this beautiful thought. I imagined all of the observable universe, the matter we can see, like planets and people, and the dark matter that we can't see, like the gravity pull on stars. I imagined all of the dark energy that permeates and accelerates our universe to its outermost edges, and when I was unable to go further, I imagined the entirety of space and time. *What is all that?* I asked myself. For a brief moment, it took shape. And I saw that it, and all it contained, was inside the mind of a great conductor. *Perhaps I, too, am being imagined*, I thought. When I was a young girl, I used to think about our universe as a matryoshka doll. Matryoshka dolls, also known as nesting dolls, are a set of wooden dolls decreasing in size that sit one inside the other. I once had my own set and spent many days opening and closing the hollow dolls, being most fond of the tiniest doll that would fit inside of the rest. If I were to play with that same set today, I suppose I could arrange all of the dolls in sequence, with the tallest doll standing as our universe and the other dolls inside acting as galaxies, orbs, and other entities. That would be one way to look at the universe, with the boundaries we've created, where we can see how everything flows and works together. Like when a leaf falls from a tree; it won't struggle to fall at a quicker or slower speed than the wind, but will simply fall in rhythm with the air's current. A flight of birds or a school of fish will move as one, just as babies' heart rates will entrain to that of their mothers, and if we swing two pendulum clocks on a wall at different rates, they will eventually end up in unison. In this same way, we can see communities of like-minded people thinking, creating, and dressing similarly. Like the leaf, they flow and congregate in each other's currents. The universe is a marvellous system of smoothly flowing information. What, then, do you suppose, contains our universe outside of the matryoshka dolls? This is what the universe is asking us every day, mostly through its rhythms in nature, art, and music. It whispers to us in our dreams and when we look up at the stars. It is the Moonlight Sonata, speaking to us in a wordless language. Yet, we think and behave inside of the boundaries, ignoring the deep sense inside of us that what we think is real may not be at all. The late philosopher and poet Friedrich Nietzsche referred to us as mighty geniuses of construction -like spiders -spinning delicate conceptual material first manufactured from ourselves. We understand a flower to be a flower because of the name and meaning we have given to it; that is a flower, this is a chair, and so on. The essence of the flower, however, if we were to look at it without having a name or meaning for it, would be incomprehensible. Consider more complex concepts, such as time, love, success, or death, without the names and meanings we have given to them. Think about your own essence without the name and meaning that was given to you. We exist alongside the elusive truth of our universe, and when we haven't yet learned all of the meaning, we simply experience this truth through our senses. With this comes the freedom you may recall as a child waking up on a summer day; when we could feel the promise of endless possibility, and didn't have to learn it. There is this notion that once children become adults they will *know*. The truth is, children know -adults *forget*. In a universe that's so vast and impossible to understand, having a confined and collective understanding creates a sense of comfort, *a forgetting*, for us all. From the moment we wake up to the moment we fall asleep, we autopilot our lives to keep everything safe and known. Some of us have children of our own now, a job, neither or both, but we all have flat screens, radios, or other devices to comfort us from -*what*? We have routines that follow a predictable schedule -and we consume videos, books, or podcasts to think and talk about our daily routines with the people around us -*why*? What is that thing, that place, or feeling that we all want? It may be more time or money; a house or vacation; peace or happiness; but these are illusions that we have forgotten are illusions, and the reason why, Nietzsche explained, we sometimes think that we must be dreaming when our spider-like world of concepts becomes torn by art. It removes us from our world of collective understanding and places us in a world of dreams, beauty, and wild artfulness. You may sense this while looking at a painting, or when listening to a symphony, or staring out at the ocean. There you are, a tiny doll inside of a much larger set of matryoshka dolls, with a masterful consciousness connected to it all and a sapient intuition about what may lie outside of the boundaries. I have dreamt of the sun swallowing the Earth, floods rising to the building tops, and bright red skies. I have looked into the eye of a whale and have felt its soul. I have stood in front of a glistening pond with a quietness so deafening that it startled me awake. Indeed, we belong to something outside of our understanding. There is no matryoshka doll for the source of consciousness that contains the universe; it lies outside the boundary. To get as close as possible, pay attention to the smallest details, using all of your senses in every moment. You will hear it in your dreams and in a conch placed up to your ear. You will see it through the rising of the sun and in the eyes of a child. You will smell it in your old memories and new adventures, and you will taste it in your food and in your blood. Feel for it in your chest and in your hand sweeping across blades of grass. Allow it to seep through you, and remember that you are and always have been a part of its infiniteness. Slow down your days and movements to acknowledge and honor the omnipresence that you are a part of. Once you awaken to this and realize that you, too, are as breathtaking as the sun, as powerful as a raging flood, as bright as the sky, and as spirited as a whale, you may one day stand beside a pond and hear the stillness of your soul. When that happens, you will see that you are intricately linked to everything, and that the power of the universe is, in essence, the power of *you*.

First Principles
The Power of You

One of the greatest discoveries you can make is that you are not merely a child of your parents but a child of the universe. When a star blows apart, all of the elements inside of it are swept out into space so that a new generation of stars can form from those elements. Once they die, they are swept out once again in a galactic chemical evolution, eventually leading to planets and, in our case, life. We see similar occurrences in nature, when a fire rages across hilltops only to form even stronger forests, or when volcanoes explode and seep lava into the ocean, only to become new land. We see it in ourselves when cells migrate in the body to grow new tissue or to heal a wound, and just as a grandfather dies and leaves behind his legacy, a baby is born into infinite possibility. Discover this more closely for yourself. When staring out of an airplane window, look down for the winding rivers that open to the mouth of the sea; the veins and arteries running through our planet that keep everything alive in an endless flow. Turn over your wrist and think of the veins and arteries that run through you, keeping everything alive in an endless flow. Go out for a walk and look up at the trees. Look at the branches and treetops and how they resemble the bronchioles in your chest cavity. Take a deep breath and ponder how the oxygen that leaves the tree gets absorbed by your lungs, and the gas that leaves your lungs is absorbed by the tree. And as you lay in bed at night, close your eyes and feel for your heartbeat. Reflect on a universe that began with no iron at all, and through stars forming, dying, and exploding, it now resides deep inside of our hearts.*

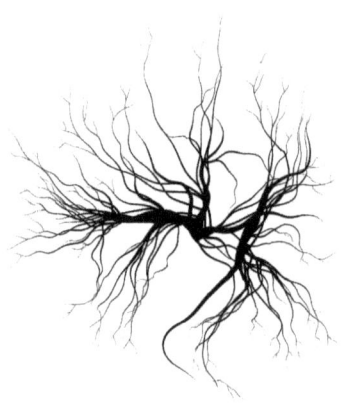

I once read about the late plant biologist Cleve Backster who conducted various experiments on plant cells in the mid-1960s. In one of his experiments, Backster hooked up a plant to a polygraph instrument and observed the recording pen move rapidly to the top of the chart as he thought about burning its leaves. In Backster's experiments on human cells, he would take white cells from a donor's mouth and place them in test tubes. He would later observe the cells responding electrochemically to the donor's emotional states while that

*(Tedx Talks: Tom Chi 2016)

donor wasn't anywhere near the building and, in some cases, in a different city. The story was a reminder for me that we are forever linked through a spaceless and timeless void, and it is in this void, in the deep fissures that form visceral tunnels between us and the cosmos, that consciousness may have sprung. Perhaps in our own dark matter, where glial cells communicate in waves, spreading from one cell to all others in an area hundreds of times their size, as if all of the universe were in us to observe. What magnificent and robust beings we are, encapsulated in an ever-changing flow of energy, information, and intelligence. It might be difficult to imagine yourself beyond the physical form, but if you hold your hand out in front of you, you may see it for what it is; a collection of atoms that have resisted being pulled apart in a chemical bond. Look for a photo of yourself from one year ago and consider how the particles that form close to the entirety of your body are now gone. Yet, your essence remains. What are you, really? Several years ago I found myself asking that very question. It was during a painful miscarriage, when a doctor was explaining the gravity of the situation to me. She explained that while a heartbeat could still be detected, the fetus was no longer growing and would eventually die. I struggled to understand what I was hearing. When asked if I wanted to empty the contents of my uterus, I declined, choosing to let nature take its course instead. Each week I would return for an ultrasound and would be told the same thing, "There's still a heartbeat," even though the ultrasound would show everything around the fetus slowly breaking down. Eventually, the form of a fetus could hardly be seen at all, and after several weeks, I remember the doctor looking at me with a pained look on her face. She couldn't understand why I didn't want the procedure, but I didn't believe it was my choice to make, when that heart would stop beating. So I walked around like that, wondering and waiting, until finally the heart had stopped, before shedding itself from my body after three months of anguish. I don't have any explanation for why I endured that for as long as I did, other than my unchanging agreement with nature that the heart is sacred. It is an organ so beautiful and complex that it not only feels and discerns, but learns and remembers as well. Just as the energy of our planet radiates from its core outwards into space, our hearts radiate their own energy field into the space around *us*. There is a frequency in life to which it connects, connecting us not only to others, but to the source energy of everything. Indeed, you are a celestial entity, an energy system mirrored with the energy systems in nature, and you are powerful beyond belief. You are not John or Samantha with the sad human story. Step outside of your mind and body and you will see that you are a physical manifestation of pure consciousness, working its way through time and space with the heart as a gateway. Imagine your heart, and the hearts of everyone you know, placed side-by-side on the ground. Imagine seeing the hearts of everyone you don't know and take a step back -a world without physical bodies, only billions of hearts that connect through vibration and memory. If you could travel to space and take a satellite image, some hearts would appear sick, while others would appear vibrant, each moving in different directions. Float further away, and what once looked like hearts would now look like a collection of cells, some lost or dying, others synthesizing or multiplying. What do you suppose makes the difference? Pick up your own heart and look around. Ask yourself when you have felt most lost and when you have felt most alive. In either of your answers, was the heart of another being not involved in some way? Pick up the hearts of everyone you know and think for a moment. A parent? A lover? Perhaps an old boss? Now pick up the hearts of everyone that you don't know. A cashier? A restaurant server? Maybe that kid in school whose name you've forgotten, but words you haven't? There is a space between everything, yet everything is connected. From the space between galaxies to the space between planets, the space between us and the atmosphere, to the space between us and each other. Everything, like cells in a petri dish, is connected, and so the power of you becomes, in essence, the power of *others*.

First Principles
The Power of Others

On an ordinary night in the midst of winter, life as I knew it had changed forever. With my heart vice-gripped in pain, I remember getting up from my chair to walk up the stairway towards my bedroom. I glanced at the framed photographs of my family along the way, tilted slightly like the compromised silk of a spider's trailed safety line. *This web had been energetically costly*, I thought. I tried to place the people in my life while my spinnerets extruded over the years. I knew what life was for me, but what was it for them? Recall Nietzsche; we build worlds and dreams for ourselves, sliding nicely into our roles, committing to sports clubs and baking cupcakes, cutting down Christmas trees, and buying puppies. Spiders we are as we build our lives. Sometimes we're so busy building, protecting, and perfecting our spectacular web when along comes the cottage owner sweeping his eavesdrop and severing us from it all. Nothing makes sense when silk is strewn across the porch. Sometimes, when we build again, it becomes clear that we were building in the wrong place, and we have only the cottage owner to thank. We can think of the people who have hurt us the most in the same way. Instead of holding on and trying to gather all of the silk, we can begin to see those who we feel have wronged us as being the teachers of our soul, and in the same way, we have had much to teach them. Of course, we can't always understand what our soul is doing as it traverses space and time in this way. Its motives lie deep in the unseen channels of our subtle bodies; invisible energies of spirit, thought, and emotion that govern every aspect of our well-being. When we hold love and compassion in our hearts, we flow through each of our bodies freely and are coherent in our lives. When we hold anger and resentment in our hearts, our bodies become blocked and we become sick. How many people do you carry with you? If I could put a kaleidoscope up to your eye for a moment, you would see a colorful and blurred mosaic of your parents, siblings, extended relatives, friends, doctors, teachers, and strangers. From the nurse who first held you the day you were born, to a high school coach or an intimate lover, you've collected an amassment of experiences and memories, both positive and negative, that have not only shaped your beliefs and interpretations, but have stayed with you in the form of pain or fear for a lifetime. To understand this more deeply, ask yourself, *How have I learned to forgive?* Many of us have learned what it means to forgive by withholding our hearts until it can be agreed that something wrong has happened, by fixating on the past, and chaining those we blame to debts that can never be repaid. True forgiveness, the kind that can free us, seems only concerned with the present moment. It is compassionate, accepts humanness, and breeds grace consciousness; everything is as it should be, because we are always learning about ourselves through our experiences and relationships with others. If we fear abandonment, for example, we might attract someone likely to abandon us, or if we lack empathy toward others, we might attract highly empathetic souls who can unearth our pain. At the soul level, we get exactly what and who we need for our spiritual growth, and how we interpret this can affect whether we are experiencing our life as a painful or joyful one. For every person that you carry with you, how much do they weigh? Are you looking backwards? Or are you existing here and now with gratitude in your heart. Reflect on how different it might feel if you could think about the person who has caused you the most pain looking into their own kaleidoscope. Suppose you could feel as much sadness for them as you feel for yourself. This isn't always so easy to imagine. I don't know what it is like to lose a family member or to know murder or malice the way that some do, and I cannot find any value in the abuse or harm of a child. For some, the weight is so heavy that it leads to bitterness and sometimes atrocious acts, while for others it leads to forgiveness. How does a parent who loses their child to violence go on to form a national foundation to help protect children while other parents live frozen in time? In less grievous cases, how do some divorced couples remain friendly while others never speak again? Why do some corporations flourish and make incredible changes in the world while others are floundering with poor reputations? I believe the answers share something in common in that every circumstance carries a collective vibration, where people can experience high frequency energy, such as love and joy, alongside low frequency energy, such as pain and fear. At some point, it must become a resilience or readiness, to open one's heart towards a more buoyant existence. The grieving parent finds strength in other parents who have survived the same, while the divorced couple who remain friends learn from leaders in personal development, and at its highest level, the flourishing corporation creates a culture of abundance, not scarcity, for all its employees. No matter what the circumstances are, when we work to unblock our bodies and live in our highest vibration possible, it appears that we are able to connect to a collective consciousness that pushes us towards our more significant purpose. To have a meaningful existence, then, would be to clear the obstructive energy from our hearts, as much as we can, to better tune into the energies of others, and, ultimately, to the source energy of everything. As a thinking being, this is an ill-fated expedition. We interpret events that unfold before us based on logic, but logic springs from our mental body alone. Instead, focusing on our more primal abilities would be wise. As a being of heart consciousness, we behave more like a rare sea jelly, relying on our nervous system to sense our way around the currents of life. Like antennae, our subtle bodies tune to the bodies of others, with an innate ability to heighten our awareness and mediate essential aspects of the energies around us. When we enhance this ability in ourselves, we gain a much deeper ability to empathize, communicate, and connect with others. After all, when standing across from another soul, all that is *is* because of the energy occurring in the space between. Like a feedback loop, encoding into fields that bind us to eternal planes of existence; you, me, and all of humanity engaged in an energetic exchange occurring nowhere other than the space between everything. Now, don't you think it's time you learned how to fly?

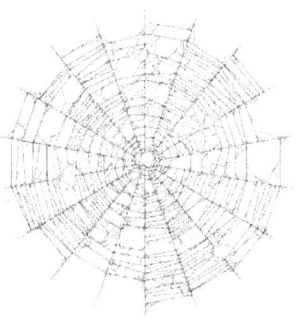

Part 2

Getting off the Ground

Home Base
Life in the Troposphere

A bird carries nothing. They are light and free from the suffering, like a winged version of our deepest longing. Yet, we go through life ignoring them.

I like to think that every human belongs to a bird in the sky. Perhaps they are carriers of the soul, celestial messengers of some kind. How wonderful to see life from *up there,* to rise above the chaos and hear nothing but the wind. Mellen-Thomas Benedict, an artist who went through an extraordinary near-death experience in 1982, says nothing of the birds. His description of what he learned through his experience, however, has confirmed for me some of my deepest intuitions about life. Following his experience, Benedict described a grid around our planet where each of our higher selves are connected. He described the higher self as a conduit, an oversoul part of our being that connects to the source of everything. Benedict explained that the bright white light that people often refer to near death is the higher self matrix. It is so brilliant because every human on Earth has a higher self. How beautiful. I suppose my bird hunch isn't so preposterous after all. Of course, we can't physically fly like a bird, but I've learned that we can fly inward as we pass through the ethereal layers of our mental and spiritual growth; that by tapping into the atmosphere inside of us, we can train ourselves to transition from a heavy state of accumulation to a weightless state of freedom. Our home base, then, is where we are heaviest. It is the default setting for all of our subconcsious thought and behavior patterns, where our life narrative takes shape, and where we preoccupy ourselves with the things that weigh us down. It is here where we feel stuck in our circumstances, while we secretly yearn for more. We go through life unaware of our home base for a long time, utterly oblivious to the power inside of us to consciously examine, explore, and re-create it.

I once habituated to a peculiar pattern of binging and purging on just about anything. Food, money, love -you name it. The amount of food that I could consume in one day is astonishing. I would tell myself *I'm not stuffed enough,* even though I could feel my skin stretching at the seams. This binging would go on for days or weeks and would always, without fail, be followed by days or weeks of strict purging in the form of exercise or food restriction. At the same time, I would copy the behavior with money. I would stretch my bank account at the seams, filling my life with vacations, live sports, home decor, or beauty products. I would consume all things desired until I no longer could, and for the next several months,

I would try to see just how quickly I could recover from it all. I would pay down my debt, sell old items online, or loan hop until everything leveled out. Of course, I could never get ahead this way, but it would serve its purpose of satisfying that driving need inside of me to feel either full or empty. It wasn't until mid-life that I came to understand how I could feed and starve myself of love in the most self-sabotaging way. It was a *human* consumption, where I would lose myself in my relationship, fixating on people and problems, until it absorbed all of my energy and left me exhausted. I would ignore or rationalize disappointments all in exchange for some emotional gratification. The worse things became, the more I would try to fill it with happiness -like filling a pail full of holes. Eventually, what once appealed to me would feel like a burden, and with my own health at risk, I would aptly play my part in burning the relationship to the ground. The pattern was pervasive. Whether it was food, money, or love, I would perpetually cycle back and forth between the sensation of filling and emptying. There was either a heaviness or a lightness to my life, an elusive *in-between* I could never stay in long enough to feel satisfied. As I grew more conscious of the pattern, I could see its reflection inside of me; a long and complicated dance between experiences of pleasure and pain. I remember thinking to myself, w*hy would I ever move toward the feeling of pain?* In exploring that question and the questions that followed, I finally came to understand and manage my patterns in a way that was self-compassionate, forgiving, and even humorous at times. I could see that whether I was moving towards pleasure or pain in my life, I was always, in some way, attempting to connect with myself, to feel a sense of comfort or control. How we relate to ourselves and others comes from how we learned to connect to ourselves and others growing up. It's how we learned to manage our thoughts and emotions, interpret circumstances, and shape ourselves over time. We go through most of our lives allowing ruminating thoughts to devour our true selves and to form our life narrative -*stories* about who we are, who the people in our lives are, and what the world *should* be like. Through our life narrative, we become very attached to who we say we are and the way we need things to be, and we begin to weave a very intricate, yet delicate, web. You, the spider, dead center in the middle of your web, what does it look like? What are your anchor points? What needs to happen in your life to keep the bridge and frame threads intact? Who are you if it falls? I only played wife on my web. I played mom, and I played teacher. I played daughter, and I played sister. It wasn't until my perfect web broke apart that I could see it for what it was. A web that I had been weaving, all based on a life narrative that would keep me trapped in silk spirals for as long as I kept the ruse going. Except I wasn't seeing this from the perspective of a masterful spider. I was free. I destroyed the web, and I now had a birds-eye-view.

One of my early childhood memories, age three or four, is of me lying prone on a gentle slope in the sun, while blades of grass were being sprinkled on my bum by a boy of the same age. It was the late seventies, no adults present, just the sound of cicadas and the smell of the earth. I learned as early as preschool that both the rays of the sun and the affection of boys felt nice. I reciprocated the grass, of course, with both of us eventually being noticed and whisked apart, pants halfway down our tiny legs. During that time, I was an omnipotent presence. I would talk to my spirit self, dig up fat worms, race caterpillars, and stare a long time at sparrows motionless on the road. I never hurt anybody, never wanted to hurt anybody, and was unhurt by others. As a child, I lived in rhythm with the world around me and can still recall the sights, smells, and sounds of a blissfully innocent existence. I was part of a Greek nuclear family who immigrated from the U.K. when my mother still carried me. I grew up with my sister, who is two years older, and several extended relatives who also immigrated and settled in Canada along with us. For the first seven years, we lived in Dundas -*the valley* -now a community in the city of Hamilton on the western edge of Lake Ontario. This area's landmarks and street names epitomized my early years: Pleasant Valley Public School, Skyline Avenue, Bumblebee Forest, and Sanctuary Park. Life back then was one Beatles hit after another. While examining myself from this early backdrop, I asked myself two questions: *When did my struggles begin?* And *What are the patterns I've consistently repeated in my adult life?* Like many, I discovered those struggles and patterns deeply rooted in my early relationships. While growing up, for example, my interactions and understanding of boys and men evolved in such a way that I felt pain in a relationship was both normal and acceptable. Beginning in preschool, and in no way extraordinary, my first exposure to the vulnerable feeling that violence evokes in us was when a dreadful little boy once told me that he was going to open up my head and eat my brains. However innocuous the event may seem in context, the first physical encounters in primary school soon followed, which again may appear as the typical soft knocks of childhood, but are nonetheless relevant. Some of these physical encounters include being struck in the face by a boy when walking home from school, whipped for fun with wet J-clothes by male cousins, and pinned up against a wall by a strange boy who wanted to rub my thigh. Most vividly, I remember a temperamental neighbor who would watch my sister and I before school. He once lifted me and swung me over his shoulder before whacking my ass hard for spilling milk on his living room floor. Thus, by the time I was seven years old, and perhaps by my backside alone, I had come to understand, in a seemingly inconsequential way, that boys were a source of both pleasure and pain. It is our initial caregivers, however, who (aside from what is in our nature) can influence and shape our patterns most. Shortly before my eighth birthday, we left the valley and moved into the central part of the city. My parents found a century-old home on Eastbourne Avenue, where the streets reeked of cherry coming from the Lifesaver factory over on Cumberland. On any given day you could hear the sound of St.Pete's bells tolling off of Main Street, sometimes drowned out by the sound of multiple sirens. My father, who was the strong, silent type, never said much when I was growing up. When he did speak, I hung onto every word, and when he didn't, I did everything I could to get his attention. He was a constant presence in my life, who always provided for and loved me, but wasn't communicative in the way that I craved as a young girl. Although I have fond memories of being with him, there was an impenetrable wall that said *you must work for the love and affection of a man*. I would constantly try to do or say things that would get a reaction from my father, but it never broke the wall down. It was a pattern I would carry into adulthood, accepting walls as a form of love, while steadfastly building walls of my own. During these same years, I found myself contending with the magnificent force of my mother; a beautiful, complex, and incredibly giving woman whose pain I felt was always carefully masked by her need to control her world and the people in it. For all the attention I lacked from my father, my mother would naturally make up for with food and affection. To this day, she would do anything for my sister and I, yet, her control over what went into and out of my body perhaps laid the groundwork for my relationship with it -and by this, I don't mean the typical frustration a parent might have when their child doesn't eat enough fruits and vegetables. I once threw up in my bowl of oatmeal and (God love her) had to eat it anyway. By the time I entered sixth grade, I was very adept at controlling my food, and by the time I was in eighth grade, I was making out with boys on the basement stairs of my best friend's house. That's life. Parents are simply the people who came before us, and they carry narratives in their hearts that have influenced and shaped who they are long before they impart anything on to us. Perhaps as a young girl, my mother was medicated with food when her mother had died, leaving her at the age of five; and when my father, age ten, had discovered his father deceased on the kitchen floor, perhaps he found less use for words in his life. I was by no means unloved or deprived of rich, positive memories growing up. My parents nurtured me as a sensitive and imaginative child who was introspective and who loved to create. Some of my favorite moments I can recall were when I was alone in my room writing or *making* something. It was only during my pubescent transition between middle school and high school, when there was a career shift for my parents, that I suddenly and most unpreparedly became a latchkey kid. Rather than continuing my creative trajectory as expected, I relished and ran wild with my new freedoms, inexplicably becoming the poster child for all parental nightmares. There's no pretty way to put it. I was into everything terrible for me, and my walls were massive. I lost my virginity in the most unloving way and was regularly binging or starving myself of food. When my attendance at school eventually fell to the wayside, it seemed nothing could stop this runaway train. There were periods, however, when my higher self would attempt to show itself. I was reading '*Love*' by Author Leo Buscaglia and books on Zen and Buddhist philosophy. I joined a local theater club and tried to make new friends, and I would sit and write poetry. Still, by the time I was seventeen, a vortex of impulsive decision-making brought me to my first cash job at a popular nightclub, in what would come to define the end of my adolescence and catapult me into the next stage of my life. I ultimately left Hamilton to live in Toronto with who would become my first husband in an abusive, alcohol-infused relationship that would span the next fourteen years. The little girl in me, who once felt at peace with herself and the world, was now overshadowed by a young woman well on her way down a path of self-treachery. By the time I had entered adulthood, my home base -or default setting -was to either seek pleasure or to protect myself from pain, and for many years, like a self-fulfilling prophecy, the pattern would permeate all areas of my life -in the way that I ate food, the way that I spent money, and the way that I would react to people and everyday situations.

It had taken over two decades and a life-altering event in my forties to finally see my patterns and accept that something needed attention in my life. Thankfully, between the anger, sobbing, and gasping for air, I became curious about how I had arrived at this point. Curious about what I was projecting to the world versus what I felt inside, and wondering why they weren't the same. I began to think about my life narrative, in the way that I could for a character in a book, and I realized that our narratives are constructs built on memories, words, and feelings; a pile of emotions -and the meaning given to those emotions -for twenty, thirty, or forty years. They are skeletons of our past dressed in the latest fashions; an utterly meaningless daily meandering that controls everything we think, say, and do. People don't want to look at their narrative from all sides: the hero, the villain, the victim, the extra. Instead, the mind deceives us. It paints a brush over our life and says, *"I've been through some things,"* in an intriguing way. I've always felt it'd better to be curious. To challenge the stories we tell ourselves and others, because challenging those stories -ideas about who we are or why we do the things we do -creates the space that is necessary for us to gain a bird's-eye-view. It's precisely that space, or separation, that invites us to see and change our patterns. I spent a year piecing together my narrative from the very beginning. I asked myself hard questions, pouring myself into books on personal development and spiritual growth. I went to weekly support meetings, leaned on close friends and family, and tried my best to gain an understanding, to heal, and forgive. When we decide to look inwards and connect to ourselves in this way, there comes a moment when we can see that we are our own most valuable resource. Amid my most profound and sorrowful pain, I slowly began to remember who I am and what I love. I began writing, painting, and bike riding -doing all of the things I loved to do as a little girl -and I took care of myself in ways that no one else could. I ran hot baths and lit candles, brought fresh flowers home, and enrolled in courses and workshops to embark on something new. Then, when I truly understood and took responsibility for the choices in my life, when I finally felt a sense of acceptance, peace, and compassion, I did something remarkable; I forgave myself. I forgave myself because I had not only reunited with who I am beyond any story or judgment, but I had fallen deeply, madly, roaringly in love with myself while looking in the mirror. I learned how to see others beyond any story or judgment and more readily forgave them as well. When something breaks in our life and shatters our sense of reality, we have a choice to either look at ourselves or to look at others. Looking at ourselves will always give us the power to change something, opening a new and more joyous world for us, while looking at others will forever hold us in a loop of suffering. In fact, a life without self-awareness, without a burning desire to grow and develop beyond our current circumstances, is an adequate definition of misery.

We look to our home base when we're ready to take stock; to look at all of the choices we've made, and to give an honest evaluation of where we are today. One of the simplest ways to do this is to look around and assess the accumulation in our life. Accumulation is what we can see and feel as a result of our patterns. It might look like a messy house, compulsive eating, or frequent issues in our personal or professional relationships, but we can never take flight with accumulation in our life because it's a profound heaviness in our hearts. Think deeply for a moment. Do you work for a living? Or do you truly live through the work that you do. Have you ever raised your voice to a child or thrown something at a lover? Have you accepted mental or physical abuse from someone? How many things are in your home, garage, or closet? What do you turn to when you feel overwhelmed, anxious, or afraid? Many of us have unfulfilling jobs, strained relationships, or a pain that hasn't healed, and it isn't uncommon to find some kind of outlet -whether it's food, alcohol, or tabloid news -to try to escape the pain somehow. When we operate mindlessly from a home base that hinders us like this, we frustrate easily, holding on to anyone or anything that has crossed us. We're unhappy with the job that we're in, or we struggle with our daily systems and feel overwhelmed with the little things. We always feel like we aren't doing enough or don't have enough money or time to feel successful, and we view life as unfair. On the other hand, when we operate from a home base that helps us, we default to love and forgive quickly. We see life as beautiful and don't waste time holding grudges towards anyone or anything. We have balance in our lives and are happy with our daily work and rituals. It's not that there's no struggle, but the meaning that we give to the struggle leaves us with hope, not despair. Don't wait until something shakes your world to begin to look around and see the heaping piles -the accumulation -all around you. Standing in the middle of that ransacked room, I invite you to see what needs to go in your life narrative, to do a complete inventory, and to begin to shed the weight. Once you've examined your home base, you will develop the power to recreate it and grow beyond where you are today. A new home base can open you up to a world of possibilities, a strengthened relationship with yourself and others, improved health, and a greater sense of peace and purpose. When this happens, the accumulation will gradually shed, and you will begin to feel, perhaps for the first time in your life, *airborne.*

Accept & Let Go
Chapter Companion

In the previous chapter, *Home Base*, I set out to understand my own story as a story; how my experiences, thoughts, and beliefs intertwined to create a lifetime of circumstances, drama, and accumulation. Putting our story to paper is not only cathartic but a necessary first step towards greater self-awareness. When we put our reflections to paper we form connections in our brain that can lead to concrete changes in our lives. This first exercise invites you to take inventory of your life -the good, the bad, and the ugly. Taking a long look in the mirror is what begins the hard and often humbling work that can lead to a life transformation. Make the time to write your story -not the story you've always portrayed or wanted people to think -but your actual story, as if the walls were watching. Many of us hold the deep sense that we are being guarded by some kind of entity our entire lives. Whatever your beliefs are, write as if there is an entity who has been with you from the very beginning and is now reading your story. There is nothing you can hide. I would go for long periods reflecting on the words I had written, living my life and sitting with it, sometimes for weeks or months, before realizing that I needed to go back and dig deeper. It's all part of the journey. Don't leave undesirable parts out. Ask yourself if you're omitting things and why. Think about viewpoints and circumstances. Edit and revise your story until it is something true of your human experience; that if someone were to find it after you die, it would be an accurate reflection of your experiences, choices, and outcomes.

12 key phrases to get you started:

1. I was born to (parent names)

_____

2. I was raised by (caregiver names)

_____

3. My siblings are (siblings names)

_____

4. I lived in (place/town/city you lived in growing up)

_____

5. The most vivid thing I remember in my earliest days (0-5) is:

_____

_____

_____

6. The most vivid thing I remember from elementary school is:

_____

_____

_____

7. The most vivid thing I remember from high school is:

_____

_____

_____

8. My relationship with my mom was:

_____

_____

_____

9. My relationship with my dad was:

_____

_____

_____

10. The key events in my 20s included:

_____

_____

_____

11. The key events in my 30's included:

_____

_____

_____

12. The key events over the age of 40 included:

_____

_____

_____

Once finished, reflect on the following 3 questions, and provide an answer in <u>one sentence</u>. You may want to use a separate writing pad or journal while reflecting on the questions. Work through several variations before creating a sentence that reads right and true for you.

1. Who am I in my current reality?

_____

_____

_____

2. What is a recurring pattern in my life?

_____

_____

_____

3. Where did I make life-altering choices?

_____

_____

_____

Sphere of Fear
Life in the Stratosphere

"Ultimately, we know deeply that the other side of every fear is freedom." Marilyn Ferguson

I've been afraid for as long as I can remember. It began as a knowing of sorts. The kind of dread one feels when lying in darkness as a child. There were always the creaks and growls typical of a century-old home that I could hear as I lay frozen in my bed, but it was the vacuity of night -the nothingness -that left me terror-stricken to the bone. Eventually, I can't be sure of when, I was no longer afraid of the darkness. I had discovered instead the dotted stars one can see behind the eyelids, and with my eyes closed I would practice shape-shifting the dotted stars into ever-changing images. I took enormous comfort in my ability to create things with my mind that no one else could see, and that had unwittingly become my lifelong strategy for falling asleep. To this day I find refuge in the light dancing behind my eyes until the sun beseeches them open. One could say it was this ritual that quelled my fear of darkness for good, or the repetition of relief that the morning sun would bring, and there would be truth in both, but darkness isn't the only fear I've had to overcome. A child who is afraid in a darkened bedroom grows up to face other worries: *Am I going to be somebody? Am I going to meet somebody? Can I get myself out of this situation? Can I create a new situation for myself?* There isn't a soul on Earth who hasn't experienced fear in some way, and this is especially true when embarking on something new. It is that deep and guttural call for change that pushes us into the barren and dangerous part of our journey that is both fruitless and full of risk. Fruitless because we can never achieve what we desire through fear, and full of risk because we can lose more than our desires should we allow our fear to cripple us. When we begin to experience a transformation, no matter how small or tangible the changes seem, we can often feel an overwhelming urge to stick with what feels safe and familiar. It's as if we are looking down at the distance that we've risen from our home base and are now panicking at how far away and different everything seems. Many people can't articulate this feeling and want to close their eyes to it, finding release instead through self-sabotaging behaviours, procrastination, or distraction. It is here where we get caught up in ourselves and others, making excuses as to why we can't do something, or simply avoiding and filling our time with gossip or consumption -anything other than the very thing that will help us to evolve and bring us into the life that is meant for us. It's not a monster lurking in the darkness that we're afraid of as adults. It's our failure and our success, our judgment and our approval, the unknown of anything beyond our home base where we keep our eyes fixed. It's only by shifting our gaze elsewhere that the fog of fear can dissipate, and where we can begin to catch glimpses of our higher self in waiting.

    I remember looking down at my eldest daughter when she was four months old. She was lying naked in her bathing tub, staring up at the world I was about to show her. *What did I have to show her at the age of 20?* I thought. Her father -my first husband -was smoking a cigarette in the other room. He was almost twice my age, in his mid-thirties, and recently released from jail. I stroked the water over my daughter's head. It felt like young motherhood had happened in an instant, but it didn't really. I had been strewing wreckage for a good six years prior to this moment. Some could say that I lost my way, but the truth is I paved it. I skipped several months of senior high school, became pregnant, and completed my diploma while preparing for a new baby. So here I was, giving her a bath. Many of us have these moments of reflection in our lives, where we can take stock of a situation, and where the potential to take action is in all of us. When my daughter looked up at me from her bathing tub, I hadn't realized it then, but my higher self had risen to whisper into my heart, *Move. Now.* In that moment, I made a choice to change course in life and continue with my education; a choice that would begin with careful, measured steps. By the time my daughter was entering kindergarten, I had finished my first post-secondary program, affording me a salaried position at a media company in downtown Toronto. It certainly wasn't the end of my professional or spiritual journey by far, but it was that innermost being inside of me who remembered that I was a creator, a creator of anything that I wanted to create, and who remembered I was destined for more than being a young mom in a volatile relationship. No matter how challenging our circumstances become, a choice will eventually present itself, and it is our choice alone. My choice made me the artist and sculptor of my life, and there was beauty and power in that choice. Just as an artist carves away at their masterpiece, gradually removing from it and reworking each part over time, I made an artistic plan for my life and character in that moment. A plan that would eventually bring me into another mode of being, and a more sophisticated life for myself decades later. In this way, every choice has an outcome. When we shrink ourselves in fear, those choices and outcomes will keep us exactly where we are, unable to grow beyond our current situation. When we elevate ourselves in the face of that fear, those choices and outcomes will carve new paths, allowing for our growth and infinite possibility. It can take years or even decades to realize the outcome of our choices, and from the outside looking in, our lives might appear paradoxical. My twenties resembled the cluttered, mud-splattered mess of a disgruntled artist. Despite an early attempt to move out and try motherhood alone, I inevitably married my first husband and chose to stay in that marriage for nearly a decade. As a family, including a daughter from his first marriage, we settled into a home just outside of Hamilton, acquiring all of the markings of suburban life -a pool, a boat, a line of credit -everything, in my mind, a person with stability would have. I volunteered heavily at my daughter's school, eventually becoming the fundraising chair of the parent council, and each summer we would drive across Quebec, New Brunswick, and Nova Scotia in an annual vacation to the east coast. Fun and adventure fills hundreds of photographs taken during my twenties. I was also choked, punched, kicked, spit on, and called stupid, worthless, and fat, for which no photographs exist. From the beginning of that relationship to the end, I had police come to my aid half a dozen times, and once appeared in a Toronto Star feature on domestic violence, highlighting a court system saturated with young women like myself. I went through various stages of ugly, churning growth in my twenties -the kind one can rarely see while living through it -and although it may sound credulous, my most extraordinary act of courage during that time came to me after reading a morning horoscope. I still have it to this day in fact, because it spoke so directly into my heart and were the exact words that I needed to hear. The horoscope read:

> *There is a philosophical belief that says the beating of a butterfly's wings can create air currents on one side of the globe that trigger a hurricane on the other. Your words work in the same way. They are powerful. Use your influence wisely.*

It was as if, in that moment, I had suddenly regained consciousness from a decade-long slumber, uncovering a treasure in this truth that my words were indeed powerful; that I was not worthless; I had a gift, and it was what I loved to do more than anything in this world. My courage had risen with such force and purpose during that time that it was all-consuming. On the morning of my thirtieth birthday, I began researching admission requirements for McMaster University, and within weeks I was enrolled in an English Literature programme part-time. While I sensed this was the beginning of an exciting journey that would lead me into the next phase of my life, I remember feeling afraid. Rather than allowing the fear to stifle me, I forged ahead with it, focusing instead on where this journey would take me. I showed up each day and did my best, and the more I did that, the less afraid I became. I wasn't eliminating the fear -I was tempering it -the way a smith would temper a sword. We all have the power to strengthen our courage this way each day; to build our resilience against frightening situations by facing them. It is the muscle in us, the strength of our spirit, and it can be can nurtured over time. Had I stopped at an undergraduate degree and neglected to nurture this muscle in me, my life would not be where it is today. I voraciously consumed as much as possible in university, facing every fear, desire, and challenge with courage. I did hard things, things I wasn't sure that I could do, and it had the compounding effect of creating momentum and confidence in everything else that I did. I eventually entered into an honors programme, followed by a graduate programme in Education, becoming a teacher within the same year of filing for divorce. Looking back, I was in my worst emotional and spiritual health during that time in my life, but I was taking courageous steps towards immense change. Although it wasn't perfect, and I continued to make mistakes, I was somewhere new, somewhere better, and with a deep sense of pride and accomplishment, a little bit closer to my higher self.

One might assume that I had alas gone on to a life of happiness, but in our fear we are masters of disguise, concealed, in plain sight, from the troubles of our soul. We can reshape our appearance with new jobs or cars, and smile longingly in the face of a new friend, but we are just holding out -that's what we do. While embarking on my career as a teacher, I almost immediately found refuge in a new life with my second husband, whom I had met years earlier. We had both been in marriages for several years before our paths crossed again, yet it felt as though little had changed by way of our mutual fondness. After a whirlwind romance, we moved into our first home together the same year that I began teaching full-time, along with my eldest daughter and two daughters from his previous marriage. Before long, our youngest daughter was born, and our family was complete. I had come a long way from that day when I was bathing my first born many years earlier. I was now in my mid-thirties, with a strong career, building a life with a spirit kindred to my own, in a relationship that felt loving and *normal.* Like many relationships, though, it went through its fair share of peaks and valleys, and we rarely -if ever -spoke about its dark undertones out loud. It was like beams of light trying to shine through the slats of a drawn blind. It was beautiful in fragments. For years I would try to feel and project a perfect marriage and family. I ignored that maybe it wasn't perfect for everyone, that for as much love as there was, that detail needed more noticing. I ignored my husband's inscrutable energy, that I never really knew what he was thinking or wanting. I ignored that we were two people dealing with our issues through the distraction of a new life and marriage, and that I wasn't allowing myself to just be still and to heal from my previous marriage. I was maladapted to this new environment, always afraid of losing my *perfect* life. I didn't realize at the time what perfection is in a truly joyful existence with another person, or that what I was really afraid of was laying bare the pain of my past and the shame that I felt. The real beauty of our marriage -standing to this day -happened after everything had blown apart, when we had separated for a year, and when, for the first time since I was seventeen, I found myself alone. When all the noise had gone away, when I was forced to sit in the quiet of my soul and feel a fear like none other, I had finally stumbled on the thing I was most afraid of -what most, if not all of us, are afraid of at our core -the fear of being unloved and unworthy of love.

The day that I came to understand this, I was lying in a darkened room, quietly begging the universe to bring me some vestige of its infinite wisdom. With tears streaming from the corners of my closed eyes, I saw the face of my youngest daughter flash before me. A succession of images that encompassed her young life followed; her birth, her smile, her moments of sadness; and as quickly as they engulfed my mind, they began morphing into images of myself as a child. I saw someone holding me as a baby, I saw my smile as a little girl, and I saw all of it fading away into pain. The universe was holding up a mirror, and in its reflection I saw that my marriage was such a small piece of something far more significant in my life that needed healing. There's no explanation for what I saw and felt on that day. If it was a vision, it was channeled deep from within. In the months that followed, I slowly found my way back to the deep and guttural spring of joy inside of me, inside of us all, that is blameless and free. I began to take such good care of my heart and was so mindful of my true spirit that peace and forgiveness washed over me in the most powerful way. I forgave my husband for dealing with his own struggles in the way that he chose to, I forgave my first husband for the pain that he caused, and I forgave myself for the mistakes that I felt I had been making since I was a young girl. I was suddenly filled with love and compassion for everyone, including myself, and I realized, profoundly, that everyone has pain and fear manifesting in their lives in differing ways. Who am I or anyone else to determine when or how a person comes to face their pain and fear? It becomes difficult to hold a grudge from this perspective, and the most beautiful way to release yourself from the words or actions of others. I knew that in order for the fear of being unloved or unworthy to exist, we'd have to create it ourselves; we'd have to tell ourselves that we're not lovable or worthy, and that everyone else is. I knew that this couldn't be true because I understood that we've all created the same fear in ourselves with thoughts that have been filtered through pain. Our ultimate fear isn't whether we can succeed in something, or whether we can leave our circumstances behind and form new ones. It isn't whether we're going to have a good relationship or a life of happiness. Our ultimate fear is our own question of whether or not we matter. *Do I matter to people? Do I matter to the world?* There can be no genuine joy until this is resolved in us. True joy occurs when we first matter to ourselves, and when we understand, deeply, our purpose in this world. Only then can we be whole enough to add to the lives of others; to love and give freely of ourselves, as we once did as children.

The discovery led me to think about the things that I would say to myself internally, things I believed about myself, and the things I was ashamed of. I remember wondering how many of my thoughts might be inducing the fear that was preventing me from pursuing my dreams and writing a book. *Why hadn't I done that yet?* I began to think that perhaps the pain I was always gravitating towards was not only reinforcing my fear, but holding me back from something unimaginable. I obsessed over these thoughts, until one day I decided to do an experiment. First, I gathered all of my report cards from grades one to eleven and spread them across my dining room table. I then laid out some of my key childhood photographs in a visual timeline, so I could see, as much as possible, the story of my past. I looked closely at my face to remember how I felt in each stage of my life. I looked at the clothes I wore and how I was carrying myself, searching for clues into experiences I may have suppressed over time. As I did this, I couldn't help but see my daughters -all of them -and think about their own experiences. After looking at the photographs, I began to comb through each report card, reading the formal observations that were being written about me during those years. *I talked too much in class, needed to take my schoolwork more seriously, and struggled with punctuality and attendance.* I closed my eyes and began to remember the feeling of being *that* student. I wasn't bad of course -a nonconformist perhaps -but in my heart I loved to learn. When reading the observations that were written later in the year, I began to notice something. Over the course of several years, throughout elementary and high school, multiple observations given by various teachers indicated that I would always find a way to turn my circumstances around. That I was hard-working, resourceful, and showed a great amount of growth and improvement. *How could I have missed this?* My narrative about what kind of child I was started to shift. I was curious to know how this might have extended into adulthood, so I started to plot out significant events in my life: my first child and marriage, going to university, my career, my divorce, my second child and marriage, and so on. I drew a rough line graph to plot things like income, what I was reading and learning, and my general quality of life during each life stage. Surrounded by a dizzying collage of reports, photographs, and notes, everything came into focus at once. After all these years, I had been gazing in the wrong place. I would say to myself, *you dropped out of high school in grade 12*, instead of saying, *you went back and finished high school after dropping out*. I would say, *you partied too much and ended up with a child at the age of 20*, instead of saying, *you were so courageous to have a child at the age of 20*. Talking to myself in such an unforgiving way had perpetuated a fear of being unloved and unworthy of love for years. More than a decade after my divorce from my first husband, I could see how much shame I was carrying. *You're an idiot*, I would say. *You were in an abusive marriage for the better part of a decade*. When the truth was, I escaped. I escaped an abusive marriage, graduated from university, and joined the College of Teachers. Each significant event in my life had led to remarkable growth and success, yet I fixed my gaze on what I felt I had done wrong for years. Facing the possibility of a second divorce and feeling the darkness around me once again, it was clear in this reflective exercise that I was now doing what I've always done since I was a little girl. I was shape-shifting. Beyond the horizon of fear were my dotted stars, and I could create whatever I wanted for myself, so I began to write this book.

Seek Inner Courage
Chapter Companion

In the previous chapter, *Sphere of Fear*, I described how I was able to overcome fear during key moments in my life, while exploring ways in which fear helps us to grow. We don't only see this in our own lives but in the lives of people whom we admire. Take the example of American professional surfer, Bethany Hamilton, who survived a shark attack when she was just 13 years old. Bethany's left arm had been bitten off during the attack and by the time she had arrived at the hospital she had lost over 60 percent of the blood in her body. Remarkably, Bethany not only returned to her surfboard a month later, she eventually returned to professional surfing, winning several national surfing titles in the years to follow. On her website, Bethany refers to herself as a Surfer, Speaker, Mama, and *Relentless Overcomer*. Not everyone shares the same story of course, but many of us are *relentless overcomers* and we don't even realize it. We don't realize it because our identity is often rooted in shame and fear from our past. Shame for our mistakes or perceived shortcomings, and fear about things that we might not be able to achieve or acquire in life. It isn't until we can face our fears and create new positive associations with them, that we can form a new narrative and understanding of ourselves. In the first part of this exercise, I invite you to get closer to the things that you might be afraid of; to consciously feel for your fear response so that you can practice opening and releasing it. Getting closer to the things we're afraid of allows us to decrease the magnitude of our fear response over time. Next, I invite you to actively reflect on the courage inside of you. Reflecting on our courage allows us to edit and revise the perpetual narrative that keeps us frozen in time. It allows us to detach from our fear and move forward with renewed confidence.

Part 1: Get Closer To Your Fear

1. Identify an event

One of the most effective ways to diminish a fear response caused by a traumatic event is to talk (or write) about the event over and over again, in great detail, to the point of extinction. Think about a time in your life when you were most afraid. There are no limits to this; it could be an embarrassing performance, a car accident, or painful abuse at the hands of another person. It doesn't matter what it is because your fear cannot be compared to someone else's fear. If you can't think of something that's happened, try thinking about something that you're afraid of happening. Once you determine what it is for you, follow the steps below over the next several weeks or months.

2. Feel the event in your body

Begin to spend time thinking about this event during times when you're alone. While sitting or laying down, simply observe how you feel in each part of your body while thinking about the event. Where do you feel tightness? If you don't feel tight per se, which part of your body are you most aware of when thinking about the event? It might be in the jaw or throat, or it might be in your stomach or groin. You don't have to do anything here other than observe your body while thinking about the event. Over time, you will become better at tuning into this mental-physical connection.

3. Practice talking about the event

When ready, begin talking to yourself quietly about the event. It might be in the shower or the car, it doesn't matter where or how you begin talking to yourself, only that you practice releasing the event. Practice taking the event from being something that's hidden inside of you to being something that's expressed outside of you. Continue to monitor how your body feels when speaking to yourself aloud about the event. You might want to pretend that you're talking to another person about it. Are you using words that feel right to you? It's okay for the way that it sounds to change over time. There is no right or wrong way to do this; it is yours, and yours alone to tell.

4. Retell the event to others

Finally, retell and relive this event to as many people as you can. You don't need to force the conversation, and there is no timeline associated with this. Just consciously seek out as many opportunities as you can to discuss the event. You'd be surprised at how many times people talk about their fears. They may say something like, *"I'm too afraid to jog alone at night,"* or *"My daughter seems so distant lately."* The first scenario is a direct example of fear for one's safety, whereas the second scenario is an indirect example of fear of losing connection with a loved one. Listen to people when they speak. Become curious and ask questions, and see how you can share your fears and experiences.

On the following pages are some prompts to assist you. First, provide your answer. Then, put it all together by looking at the example starter statements and creating one of your own.

My greatest fear is:
- a) Dying
- b) Being alone
- c) Failing or being judged
- d) Not achieving my dreams
- e) Other:_____

This affects my life because:
- a) I'm always anxious
- b) I struggle in my relationship(s)
- c) I never finish projects that I begin
- d) I'm generally frustrated with my work life
- e) Other:_____

A time in my life when I was most afraid was when:

_____

_____

_____

This still affects my life today because:

_____

_____

_____

Putting it all together

Read the example starter statements below and use the answers that you provided above to create a starter statement of your own. You can use this starter statement when talking to yourself or others about your fear(s). This is an important first step when dealing with fear and an effective way to build accountability and connection with yourself and with others.

Example starter statements:

My greatest fear is failing or being judged. This affects my life because I never finish projects that I begin. I get excited at first and put a lot of time and effort towards something, but then when it comes time to present it, I freeze.

Or

A time when I was most afraid was when I was left alone for long periods as a child. This still affects my life today, because I have difficulty being alone and I struggle in my intimate relationships.

My starter statement:

_____

_____

_____

Part 2: Courage Collage

In this next exercise, I invite you to find several photographs of yourself that were taken during pivotal periods in your life. Look for pictures of yourself that were taken during a time that your memory naturally gravitates towards. Ideally, you would have photographs from your early childhood and high school, in addition to moments throughout young adulthood that may have been particularly challenging. We all have moments that we feel ashamed or embarrassed about, or moments that we criticize ourselves for. Look for photographs from those times, and spend time looking at them. Record the thoughts that come to mind when looking at the photographs, even if they are negative, then ask yourself, *what happened next?* There is an opportunity here to shift the narrative of your past; to rewrite your history, sort of speak, so that you can see yourself as the courageous protagonist of your own life. What have you relentlessly overcome? What were your defining choices that led to something positive in your life? When did you take action even though you were afraid? If you aren't sure where to start, refer back to the 12 key phrases that you filled out from the *Home Base Chapter Companion*. First, start with the earliest photograph of yourself, age 0-5, then choose one photo from elementary school, one photo from high school, one photo from your 20's, and each decade thereafter until you reach your current decade. Spread your photos onto a large piece of paper or digital application (roughly 5-7 photos) and beside each photo affix a sticky note or text box. Below is an example of my courage collage. For each photograph, I placed my negative thoughts in quotations and my new narrative on pink sticky notes. Take your time with this. Edit and revise your collage until it looks and feels like something true for you.

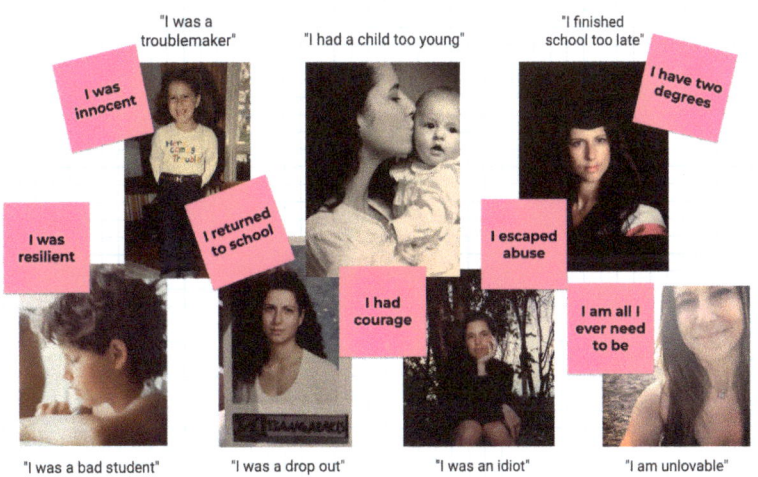

State of Being
Living in the Mesosphere

"To the mind that is still, the whole universe surrenders."
Lao Tzu

A leopard prowling through the rainforest camouflages herself with the beauty that she belongs to. Humpback whales glide over the Pacific, while nighttime crickets rub their forewings together, and you, too, have a role to play in this majestic wonder called life. It might be in the way that you stretch at the side of your bed early morning, with the sun filtering through the room, or how strands of hair will stick to your face as you walk along a windy beach. There is no *Kalopsia* in this -the delusion of things being more beautiful than they are -no Instagram posts or Tik Tok reels, only the purest form of pleasure, felt through the perception of nature itself. Some might refer to this as the sensation of *flow* or *balance*, but much more than that, it is our natural, blissful state beneath the endless hum of traffic, electronics, and chatter. In this state, we are able to match the frequency of higher energy forces, such as gratitude and love, which then shape our experiences in all areas of our life. The simple things will catch our attention, like water droplets on a leaf, or the way someone changes their gaze or expression, and we can think clearly and intentionally about the things that we want to do and accomplish. When we match the frequency of lower energy forces, such as resentment or bitterness, our experiences instead feel fast and overwhelming, where we're too caught up in the noise to notice the beauty all around us. Our emotions and attention are often misplaced onto others, and we go about life mindlessly, forgetting that we belong to the stillness like the leopard and the whale. Which state would you say you are in right now? Sometimes it might feel like we are being pulled from one state to the other each day. While other times it may feel like we are paddling through long periods in each. Learning how to consistently master our state is one of life's greatest, most rewarding endeavors. There are no public accolades for running five miles each day or packing five nutritious lunches for our children each week. No merit comes from the integrity that we hold ourselves against or the compassion that we hold for strangers. Instead, we are honing something more valuable in our quiet pursuit. This is the mesosphere of life; the space between where we currently are and where we want to arrive; and in this space is *who* we become in order to get there. The mesosphere can be seen as your training ground, where you practice, fail, and succeed over and over again until you are mentally and physically better. Better in the way that you function each day, better in the things that you pay attention to and create in the world, and better in the words that you speak to yourself and to others. Yes, the real prize in life, to be in a quiet, blissful state, is not obtained by chance or time, it is obtained by what we *do*, *think*, and *say*.

I. Exercise is spiritual

There are three principles one could adhere to should they wish to master what they do each day, with the first principle being that exercise is spiritual. It doesn't matter what it is, whether it is walking, cycling, swimming, lifting weights, or gardening, when we are moving in tandem with the energies of the universe, we are engaging in a most intimate relationship with ourselves through our body. One of my more challenging habits living in the northern hemisphere is to wake before the sun rises so that I can make it to a 6 a.m. spin class. When my alarm goes off there are eight things that I need to do to get out the door: get out of bed, urinate, wash my face, brush my teeth, get dressed, pour coffee, put my shoes on, and grab my keys. Once I'm on the road it's sometimes pitch dark, and I'm keenly aware that I haven't done this purely for the love of spinning on a bike. Much of what I know to be true of life can be found in any one of those early mornings; there are going to be good days and bad days, we need challenges to become resilient and to grow, and community is everything. In this way, what we do each day matters. How we move, when we move, *why* we move. When it comes to why we exercise, the challenge lies in first determining who decides that for us. Each new year comes with the latest winter workouts to kick-start our resolutions. We're told to shed those pounds and strengthen our glutes, as if by doing so we've achieved something great, and by not doing so we've failed. What if instead you had an agreement with yourself to be kinder and happier with your choices -to eat fruit cake for breakfast before bundling up and walking out into the cold, crisp air for a long winter walk? Come Summer we're told to get beach ready, as if by doing so we'll belong on the beach, and by not doing so we'll somehow be out of place. What if instead, you cultivated a new relationship with the beach that has nothing to do with how you look and everything to do with how you feel? Only you can determine why you are exercising. Find something you love that reminds you of your strength and humbles you in your weakness. Try climbing or paddle boarding, or sunrise walks and cool morning dips. These habits have nothing to do with the right workout, or the right number of workouts, and everything to do with what works for you, what you love, and what feels right. There's no point in trying to make it to a gym every day if the gym is the last place you want to be. Instead, move your body in ways that you love to move your body, and in places that you love to be in. What matters most is what you will be able to consistently do and improve upon. Bring this elegance into your life. Move every day, and move in a way that's purposeful, a way that reminds you that you are alive.

II. Diet is spiritual

The second principle one could adhere to should they wish to master what they do, is that diet is spiritual. I can recall becoming increasingly aware of food production when I was a young teenager. Food coming in cans, boxes, and bags left me feeling angry, trapped, and controlled. I wanted to know who was in charge, and to somehow stop the machine that I felt was consuming me. As a child, I didn't think much of it; relatives would bring me sweet treats in shiny packages, and I would give anything for a hot dog or a bag of chips at school. As I matured, I began to recognize the difference between the processed foods that I was eating and the earth-to-table foods I was accustomed to, like fresh tomatoes, or roasted lamb and potatoes that were made in traditional Greek fashion. Still, I continued to struggle with food choices throughout my adult life. The reason, unsurprisingly, had very little to do with food and everything to do with my state of being; the restriction when needing control, the binging when feeling out of control, and the self-backlash when it felt as though I had failed. I knew I should be ingesting only what's needed and only what's good, but the question would gnaw at me: *What is good?* Some foods felt good in the moment but left me feeling sick when the moment had passed. And some foods felt bad in the moment, leaving me satiated and energized after consuming them. While puzzling over this for several years, it gradually became clear what I needed to do, and why I had never been able to find the answer before. I was listening in the wrong place. I didn't need to read it in a book or on the internet, and I didn't need to memorize anything *good* or *bad*, all I needed to do was listen to what my own body was asking for and then pose a new question: *Am I in a high state or a low state?* By asking that question, I could discern whether it was my mind or my body that needed feeding, and I could vet my food choices in a new way. This made it ok for me to eat whatever I wanted because there was no shame in realizing that what was *good* is what my body was telling me that it needed. I began to notice that I often wanted processed foods when I was in a low state, and more wholesome foods when I was in a high state. Neither is good or bad, only informative. The world didn't have the answer for me because my body has always been my ultimate apothecary. I've always held the key, and so do you.

III. Sleep is spiritual

The third principle one could adhere to should they wish to master what they do each day, is that sleep is spiritual. Holding to this principle means honoring our dream state, paving the way for it, and witnessing the morning sun each day. The reason for this is simple; when we dream (even if we can't remember our dreams) we connect with our deeper selves. Our subconscious desires and fears play out as we peer into worlds that echo our feelings, decisions, and ideas. Because of this, no one can decipher the meaning of your dreams. They are unique to you, and only you carry the code to understanding them. Curious as this may sound, I once met the gatekeeper of my dreams. I had somehow reached the barren outer limits of my mind, alone and afraid, when he suddenly appeared. The dream was warm and bright as I walked along a dirt road with lush grass and mature trees all around. There were no cars or people, and I could hear no birds or insects. It was just me walking alone on this long and empty road. Suddenly, a dog appeared, followed by several more, and I became afraid. The dogs were large in size and dark in appearance, and before I could decide what my next move would be, the gatekeeper appeared. He was the survivalist type, wearing dark clothing and boots, with a bandana around his neck and head. Without words, I could see that he was aware of my presence, but he didn't look at me. Instead, he made a clicking noise that immediately led the dogs away from me and over to his side. I watched them all walk out of view before turning my head in the direction of a large, glistening pond only a few meters away. I couldn't take my eyes off the water; it was so beautiful. Then, there was a long, piercing crescendo of cicadas before everything went quiet. Both the man and the dogs were gone, and a stillness I have never felt in the waking world washed over me. The silence, swallowing me like the vacuum of space, severed me from my dream. I knew that the man I had seen was a gatekeeper and that the water I was staring into was a reflection of my solitude. It was a place in my mind that I had never reached in a dream before; a place shown to me only after I had found the way. My life changed after that dream; I knew that everything would be okay, and not by any conscious effort to think it so, but by knowing that this incredible stillness resided somewhere inside of me. How marvelous, to have this built into our being; to be yoked to the universe in this way while we sleep. Is it not worthy of honoring, that we hold the answers so precious to us? Worthy of looking forward, in ritual, to this most important time of day without distraction or noise? Worthy of rising with the sun, to reflect on all that we've learned through midnight's whisper? Soon enough, whatever your day may bring, it will come to a slumberous end, where the opportunity for transcendence presents itself all over again.

Just as there are ways in which we can master what we do each day, there are ways in which we can master what we think. Imagine standing barefoot on the edge of a cliff, with your feet sinking into the cold, damp earth beneath you. Behind you are vast empty fields that represent your past; all of the people, moments, and events in your life that have led you to the edge of this cliff. Ahead of you is the wide, open sea that represents your future; all of the possibilities, questions, and mysteries of the unknown. It is clear to see that you will be lost if you walk back towards the empty fields, and you will surely drown if you jump into the sea. All there is -all there ever is -where we can truly awaken to the life force flowing through us, is on that piece of cold, damp earth in the present moment. We often pay attention to things that have happened in the past or things that might happen in the future, but when our attention is on the past or the future we are asleep. It is only by focusing our attention in the present moment that we can be truly awake. Do you want to be happy? Try paying attention to happy things. Are you sad? Avoid paying attention to sad things. Our emotions are a direct reflection of what we are paying attention to and the meaning that we are giving to those things. When we turn our attention to the present moment, over and over again, it is like training a muscle. Eventually, the way that we view people and situations won't be rooted in past experiences or future worries, because we will have trained our mind to focus on the present moment. Begin to monitor your thoughts carefully, and you will be amazed at how often they are in the past or future, rather than the moment you are presently in. As you notice the thought, say to yourself *"I turn my attention to"* (whatever it is you are currently doing or focused on). It may be *"I turn my attention to this meal I'm cooking,"* or *"I turn my attention to my child,"* and although it may seem laborious at first, it is a crucial mastery of the mind. Imagine the power in this when considering what you want to create in the world, or perhaps your own reinvention. Imagine turning your attention to the creation of that person instead of a toxic ex-partner or gossipy friend. I have a vision board in my office wholly dedicated to what I want to create in all areas of my life. There are words to describe what I want in my relationship -words like autonomy, honesty, and loyalty -there are images of where I would like to live one day, and what I would like to accomplish. Some quotes reflect the kind of person I strive to be, and photos of people who I would like to meet one day. There are photos of myself and my youngest daughter, as well as the laminated horoscope that I cut out over twenty years ago. The entire board is a beautiful portrait of my dreams and vision for my lifetime, with the words "I am open to receiving whatever the day may bring" in the middle of it. Put to paper how you intend to fashion yourself during this lifetime and pay good attention to it. Should you find yourself living in such a way that doesn't reconcile with your creation, know that you have the power to correct it.

Mastering what we do and think, however, is of no use

if we can't master what we say to ourselves and to others. The words that we speak come first from the thoughts formed in our mind, and depending on the meaning that we give to those thoughts, our words will reflect the world that we create for ourselves. We truly speak our life into existence this way. Whether it's our relationships, work, health or overall happiness, we reinforce our world by the words that we choose to represent it. The woman who tells anyone who will listen what a jerk her husband is, is not living in a world with an amazing husband. She's choosing the narrative of the poor wife with the jerk husband, and naturally, that is what she will receive. The man who jokes about how chained he is to his wife is not living in a world with a wife with whom he feels free. He hasn't allowed that while he continues to live in the narrative of the poor husband with the ball and chain wife, and naturally, that is what he will receive. What if instead both the woman and the man made an effort to be conscious of how they spoke about the other? To use words that focus on why they love and feel grateful for each other. It is the difference between living a life where we feel fulfilled or unfulfilled in our primary relationship. When it comes to one's work life, what kind of existence is it for the man who complains of his job each day, versus the man who speaks with joy or gratitude about his work? Say you were in a job that you didn't want to do long term, and each day you said aloud "*I can't stand this job and wish I never had to come back tomorrow.*" With every tomorrow your days would become heavier and heavier, causing stress and unhappiness. What if instead, you said aloud "*I am so grateful to have a job...I can't wait until tomorrow so that I can earn more money while I work towards my dream.*" With every tomorrow your days would become lighter and lighter, causing much excitement and happiness. It is the difference between living a life where we feel motivated or unmotivated by our work. This is also true of people who say they feel fat. How can one expect to feel light if they're instructing their mind to feel fat? When we flip our words to reflect the life that we want to create, an amazing thing begins to happen; our life becomes what we want it to be. Instead of saying "*I feel so fat,*" one could say "*I'm going to eat lighter from now on.*" Instead of saying "*I feel so tired,*" one could say "*I will get more sleep tonight.*" It is the difference between living a life where we feel happy or unhappy with our overall health. Words have a biochemical effect in this way. Meaning, everything we say to ourselves affects our chemistry, and in the same way, how we interact socially affects the chemistry of others. Do you insult or ridicule people under the guise of a joke, or do you raise and compliment the qualities of those around you? Your words can be weapons or gifts, and you have the power to create the outcomes that you want to create for yourself. When you master your words, along with your thoughts and your actions, manifesting what you want in life becomes entirely possible.

State of being, then, is both our experience of life, as well as our capacity to expand and realize our greatest potential. Learning who we are when we're in a high state, and who we are when we're in a low state, and being able to recognize ourselves in both, is the awareness of self that is necessary for transformation. If we stay in a low state for too long we will inevitably fall backwards into the sphere of fear, frozen in a vicious cycle of excuses and procrastination. Try not to let resentments or bitterness linger in your heart. Try not to get caught up in the noise and negativity. Ignoring the way that your body needs to move, eat, and rest, not paying attention to the present moment, or to the words that you use, can weigh you down in self-deprecation, doubt, and fear. If, on the other hand, you can become skilled at living more consistently in your highest state, treating your body as your temple, and paying attention to what's important, time can slow down enough for the steady pulse of life to be felt; where you can feel your true grace and prowess; and where you can rise, with fierce determination, towards the next and most important layer in your ascent; the thermosphere.

Change Your Habits
Chapter Companion

In the previous chapter, *State of Being*, I discussed how the accumulation of choices we make each day, in every situation, will lead to a sum effect. Determining the sum effect of your life tomorrow, for example, depends greatly on the choices that you make today. More often than not, however, it's our environment or our circumstances that are dictating our choices. If we want any control over where those choices will lead, we need to have a vision of ourselves and our future. For several years, whenever heading into a new year, I would say to myself, *I'm not starting the new year like this*. I didn't want to spend another year living through the same old struggles, and so that is what I would say. The problem with this mantra is that it spoke only of what I *wasn't* going to do, and said nothing of what I *was* going to do. Each year stood ahead of me saying "*So what?*" Knowing what I didn't want was easy. I didn't want to be codependent; I didn't want to be stressed and unhappy; I didn't want to be unhealthy; I didn't want to be a neglectful parent; I didn't want to work in an unfulfilling job; I didn't want to be broke. Visualizing all of the things I *didn't* want, though, wasn't going to get me to what I *did* want. I wanted to be independent; I wanted to be at peace; I wanted to be healthy; I wanted to be a good parent and role model; I wanted joy in my work; I wanted financial freedom. These were all things I could apply action to and create. Eventually, with the help of a dear friend and therapist, my new maxim became, *I'm starting the new year with a new focus. A focus on who I want to be, on the life I want to have, and the steps I need to take to get there.*

Part 1: Create Your Vision

Putting a vision board in place isn't going to magically bring the vision to life, but it will help you to stay focused on what it is that you want, and who it is that you want to be in this life. When that becomes your focus, you will naturally attract more of what you want and less of what you don't want. I keep my vision board somewhere that I can see it daily. Like a mirror, it reflects back to me, and I always know whether I'm staying close to my vision, or if I'm making choices that are taking me further away from it. The previous exercise had you creating a collage based on your past, so that you could rewire your negative self-talk. The exercise on the next page invites you to create a vision for your future, using images, words, and found objects. Use the template shown as a guide.

Personal Vision Template

A Future Home	A Skill or Offering	An Ideal Relationship
What does the home of your dreams look like? A country ranch? Somewhere on the water, or in the city? Place images/ words/ objects to represent your dream home in this corner.	What is a special skill that you can see yourself sharing with others in the future (e.g., public speaking, entertaining). Place images/ words/ objects to represent your skill or offering here.	What kind of partner do you want to be and have in life? Whether you're single or in a relationship already, place images/ words/ objects to represent your dream relationship in this corner.
A Reason Why	**A Personal Mantra**	**A Current Project**
Everyone has a person, place, or thing that motivates them to keep moving towards their vision. Place images/ words/ objects to represent the reason *why* you want this vision here.	Central to your vision is your mantra. Mantras have the power to alter your subconscious impulses and afflictions. Find or create a mantra to represent your vision and center it here.	What is something special you are working on? Do you have an idea for something that excites you? Find images/ words/ objects to represent your special project or idea and place them here.
An Inspiration	**A Life Dream**	**A Spiritual Aid**
Who or what inspires you? Are there books you've read or people in the world that you admire? Find images/ words/ objects to represent your sources of inspiration and place them in this corner.	Your life dream is something you've always thought about. Usually, it's something you feel you're meant to be doing in life. Find images/ words/ objects to represent your dream and place them here.	Spiritual aids are people, places, or things (in flux) that can help guide your spiritual journey in a gravitational way. Place images/ words/ objects to represent your spiritual aids here.

*Adapted from the work of Dr. Zafire Fierro, PhD, C.Psych

Part 2: Manage Your State

In the section that follows, you will find supplementary information in the areas of food, exercise, and sleep. These references (Food For The Soul, Exercise For The Soul, and Sleep For The Soul) are especially useful since your choices in these areas can directly affect your daily state and overall quality of life. All of the information has been carefully researched, and sources can be found in the bibliography section of this book. This information is for educational purposes only and should not be taken as medical advice.

Food For The Soul

Many of the foods listed below are anti-inflammatory, detoxifying, and full of nutrients that can support your natural chemistry. Although the list isn't exhaustive, it includes over 100 incredible foods that can protect, support, and enhance the body. At your own pace, see how many of these foods you can incorporate into your everyday life. Some of the easiest ways include morning smoothies or daily salad variations with a protein of your choice. Whether you choose to experiment for a few months or adopt a new recipe for life, the point is to experiment. Your body will naturally gravitate towards what it needs and wants.

Artichokes	Squash	Pecans
Lemons	Zucchini	Pine Nuts
Avocados	Sweet Potato	Sunflower Seeds
Tomatoes	Lentils	Sesame Seeds
Lime	Cabbage	Hemp Seeds
Spinach	Lemongrass	Chia Seeds
Broccoli	Mushrooms	Pumpkin seeds
Brussel Sprouts	Jicama	Cage-Fr Eggs
Cucumber	Radish	Grass Fed Beef
Celery	Seaweed	Grass Fed Lamb
Kale	Bell Peppers	Fr-Range Chicken
Fennel	Shallots	Fr-Range Turkey
Arugula	Onion	Wild Salmon
Swiss Chard	Garlic	Black Cod
Collard Greens	Olives	Crab
Bok Choy	Almonds	Mussels
Asparagus	Walnuts	Scallops
Cauliflower	Pistachios	Shrimp
Eggplant	Macadamia Nuts	Ceviche

Dark Chocolate	Feta Cheese	Cardamom
Cacao/ Cocoa	Queso Fresca	Chili
Pomegranate	Parmesan	Basil
Cranberries	Coconut Oil	Rosemary
Blackberries	Olive Oil	Thyme
Blueberries	Cider Vinegar	Dill
Raspberries	Wine Vinegar	Cilantro
Strawberries	Raw Mustard	Chives
Acai Berry	Tahini	Cumin
Cherries	Pesto	Turmeric
Figs	Pico De Gallo	Spirulina
Almond butter	Sea Salt	Collagen
Almond Milk	Flax	Bone Broth
Coconut Milk	Flax Oil	Black Coffee
Grass Fed Butter	Cinnamon	Green Tea
Plain Yogurt	Vanilla Extract	Burdock Root
Kefir	Ginger	Dandelion Rt
Hard Cheese	Cayenne Pep	Lion's Mane
Heavy cream	Parsley	MCT Oil

Exercise For The Soul

The most intimate relationship you will ever have is with your body. Not through shame or ridicule, but through love, reverence, and encouragement. Many of us view exercise as a way to punish our body, as if it has failed us in some way, but when we do that, we only grow further away from it. It is better to grow closer to our body, to treat it with tender thoughts, words, and actions, so that we intrinsically want to strengthen and fuel it. Introducing the practice of Yoga into your life can bring you into a more wholesome relationship with your body. It can reveal to you where you are strong, and where you are vulnerable; it can teach you when to engage and when to soften; and it can give you a foundation of strength, flexibility, and balance unparalleled to any other activity. Before you attempt the latest workout craze, simply ask yourself: *what will bring me closer to knowing my body?* Can you stand in a basic Tadasana (mountain pose), and be mindful of every muscle in your body? First learn to strengthen this essential connection between your mind and your body; nurture consistency, patience, and focus at its most basic level, and you will build confidence, grit, and determination. This deeply intimate connection with yourself is what keeps you going, making you want to move and be challenged, even on your most difficult days.

Basic Asanas

The following basic asanas (postures) are perfect for beginners and known for improving flexibility and range of motion in the legs, glutes, and back muscles. These postures have a low injury risk, and can also help to release stress and tension in the neck, shoulders, and back. They are calming, grounding, cooling and supportive, and particularly beneficial for those suffering from insomnia or anxiety.

*All illustrations are the work of sketch artist, Rebecca Humble

1. Corpse Pose (Shavasana)

2. Child's Pose (Balasana)

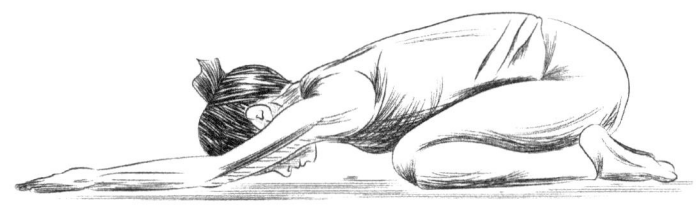

3. Bridge Pose (Setu Bandha Sarvangasana)

4. Happy Baby Pose (Ananda Balasana)

5. Cow Pose (Bitilasana)

6. Cat Pose (Marjariasana)

Beginner Asanas

The following beginner asanas are known for strengthening the core (abdominal) muscles and creating the foundation for more advanced yoga poses. These postures are grounding, as they help to improve balance and flexibility in the hip flexors, as well as build strength and stability in the legs, glutes, and Muladhara -the root chakra.

7. Boat Pose (Paripurna Navasana)

8. Downward Dog Pose (Adho Mukha Shvanasana)

9. High Plank Pose (Phalakasana)

10. Cobra Pose (Bhujangasana)

11. Triangle Pose (Utthita Trikonasana)

12. Warrior I Pose (Virabhadrasana)

13. Warrior II Pose (Virabhadrasana II)

14. Tree Pose (Vrksasana)

15. Chair Pose (Utkatasana)

Intermediate Asanas

The following Intermediate asanas hold all of the previously mentioned benefits of increasing strength, improving balance and flexibility, as well as opening the various energy channels in the body. With the challenge of more advanced postures comes the opportunity to build confidence and resilience, while attempting to master the art of stillness, breathwork, and presence.

16. Camel Pose (Ustrasana)

17. Eagle Pose (Garudasana)

18. Warrior III Pose (Virabhadrasana III)

19. Side Plank (Vasisthasana)

20. Locust Pose (Salabhasana)

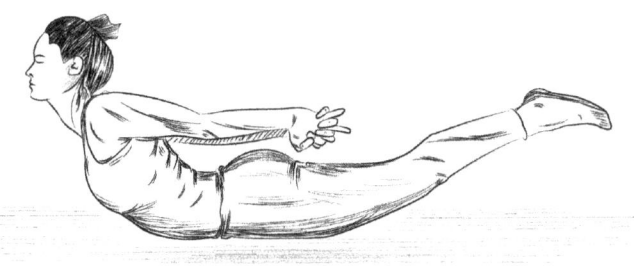

Sleep For The Soul

Sleep is the absolute foundation of your mental and physical health. If you begin to adopt these essential wake/sleep habits, every aspect of your life can benefit.

View Morning Sunlight

Try to wake up each morning at the same time and view bright sunlight within the first thirty to sixty minutes after waking. This allows the hormone, cortisol, to reach its peak early in the day, increasing your metabolism and level of focus, and setting in motion an internal timer for sleep later at night. Avoid checking your phone or computer. Instead, get outside and either walk or sit for at least ten minutes while looking towards the sun. This is the most powerful catalyst for both wakefulness and for your ability to fall asleep at night.

Increase Your Body Temperature

Try increasing your body temperature with exercise and/or cold exposure early in the morning. Cold exposure could include a cold shower, tub, or lake dip for one to three minutes. This causes the adrenal glands to send epinephrine through your bloodstream, which rapidly increases your body temperature. Even a modest amount of movement helps, such as walking, jogging, or jumping rope. Both early morning cold exposure and movement create a biological domino effect that can last throughout the day and optimize your sleep patterns.

Manage Food, Alcohol, & Caffeine

Timing and quality of food intake is important when it comes to your sleep cycle. Try to eat at the same time each day, while choosing whole foods over processed or sugary foods. Keep a food intake window of around eight to ten hours, and avoid eating large meals for at least three to four hours before falling asleep. For some, caffeine intake should end somewhere between two o'clock and four o'clock in the afternoon, and if your goal is to improve your sleep quality, avoiding alcohol altogether could help, as it greatly disrupts sleep patterns.

Practice Healthy Evening Routines

When the sun begins to descend, try to get some sunlight in your eyes. This signals your brain and body to prepare for sleep. Avoid bright artificial lights, and consider lighting candles. Take a hot shower/bath, sauna, or steam, and make your environment cooler. These are cues for your body that it is time to sleep soon, and it will naturally prepare itself. Sleeping at the same time each day (within reason), and wearing a loose-fitting eye mask can also help.

Keep A Dream Journal

If you can remember your dreams, having a dream journal may help you to strengthen your intuition in the waking world by tapping into your subconscious. As soon as possible after waking, try to capture significant details of your dream using the template below, or any template that works for you.

Date: _____

Animals I saw: _____

People I saw: _____

Places I found myself in: _____

Words I remember: _____

Numbers I remember: _____

Vivid Symbols/Objects: _____

How I felt in the dream /upon waking:_____

_____

What it means to me: _____

_____

Part 3

Experiencing Your Greatest Transformation

Self Mastery

Life in the Thermosphere

"Knowledge of the self is the mother of all knowledge."
Khalil Gibran

Some time ago, I was out having dinner with a group of colleagues, when someone at the table asked what my dream job would be. "I wouldn't have a job," I replied. "I would be a writer, living on the ocean." I knew so clearly what I would rather be doing, and yet I had never heard myself say it out loud. Isn't that the way for many of us, dreaming of how we want to be spending our lives, while quietly enduring something different each day. Being a writer and living the life of an artist isn't where my vision ended. I yearned to be financially free, calm and steady in my mind and spirit, traveling and mingling with like-minded creators. I pictured myself living in an open-air home filled with art and wind chimes; lounging in soft, loose clothing, with the roar of the ocean all around me. *Why can't I have this*? For decades I had been a giver in my role to everyone around me; a daughter, a wife, and a mother; but *this* is who I am and how I truly want to live. *Now what?* I thought. I was broke, living paycheque to paycheque, and almost fifty thousand dollars in debt. Should you ever find yourself in such a place, wondering what you can do to get from where you are to where you want to be, you're in a very good place. In other words, when you find yourself utterly discontent with your life, rejoice! This is your opportunity for transformation. Once you have come to accept who you are, and what your home base looks like; once you have courageously made it through to the other side of fear; once you have discovered what you are truly capable of in both your low and high states, you are in the thermosphere of life, where everything can align and you can begin to live through your true passion and purpose.

For many years I watched in admiration as two dear friends of mine transformed their entire life to better reflect who they are and what they value most. Parents to three young children, they sold their suburban home and hit the road to travel in a motorhome all over the U.S. and Canada. Like a struck chord, the move reverberated deep in my soul, and in many ways marked the beginning of a new chapter in my life. There was something so familiar in the beliefs that my friends held, and for a long time it was confusing not to be able to identify what was stirring inside of me. It made me look around at my life -my career, my marriage, my kids -and I remembered that before this life I had created, there was a girl who wanted nothing more than to roam the world in adventure one day. Life is funny this way. The people who come into our lives are never by accident. Some have lasting roles, others are conduits, and in this instance, my dear friends unknowingly changed the course of my life the moment they entered it. Take the time to notice what life is trying to show you. Chances are it will lead you directly to where you need to be, to who you need to become, and to what you're meant to be doing. Until then, you might describe life as stressful, because it is stressful to feel like you are not where you should be, being the person you are deep inside, doing what you were always meant to do. We say it's our relationships, our career, or our health that brings stress to our lives, but that's not it. What brings stress to our life is going against our current; losing sight of what truly brings us joy while we're busy earning degrees, finding a spouse, building a family, and paying the mortgage. I've spoken to countless people who feel stuck in lives that don't agree with who they genuinely are; businessmen who would rather be vagabonds, educators who would rather heal people, and tradesmen who would rather be artists. Following our hearts back to our true passion and purpose requires us to notice the things that move something deep inside of us. Perhaps it's that friend who quits his job to start a new business from home or a relative who suddenly takes up a hobby. Maybe it's seeing your neighbor training for a marathon each day or a colleague who's decided to travel across Europe. Whatever it is for you, take the time to notice it, contemplate how it makes you feel, and explore the possibilities in your own life. It's easy to push the feeling away as a source of discomfort, but what if you brought that discomfort closer to you instead? What if you allowed yourself to scan and scrutinize that discomfort from all sides? It's precisely that act that can help you to remember exactly *who* you are and what it is that you have to offer this world. You might say *"I would have to go back to school," "I have 3 kids,"* or *"One has to know somebody to be successful at that,"* but those are just tricks of the mind designed to protect you from the discomfort of change. The world keeps you comfortable with mediocrity, and when you accept mediocrity and let doubt stop you from creating your life as you want it to be, you are doing yourself and the world a great disservice. It needs believers. Believers are the ones you envy, the ones who live exceptionally and can tell you about their long battle and victory over doubt. Believers say, "If it's within your control, there is absolutely nothing you cannot change in your life." Close your eyes and remember when you knew in your heart that anything was possible, or when your stomach tingled with excitement at all the things you would do one day. You might hear a voice saying, *"Then reality hit,"* but the opposite is true. Doubt fuels our self-fulfilling prophecies, and the child-like belief we all have inside of us that anything is infinitely possible is what fuels our wildest dreams.

One of the most remarkable ways that we can make a meaningful change in our lives is to shift the way that we think about time. Time is commonly measured in blocks or units, but it can also be measured by our experience. We often struggle with finding time in our day, not because there isn't enough of it, but because of how we have come to define and measure it. We may say, "I have to work between eight o'clock in the morning and six o'clock at night, so where am I going to find the time?" To which one could respond, "You have between eight o'clock in the morning and six o'clock at night." If we're at work all day, and that's where our time is going when we'd rather be doing something else, then yes, we have lost time and time has won. This is because we have measured time by hours, and not by experience. What's more, we've learned to define time as an experience we have no control over, versus an experience that we have control over. I am fortunate to be working with young children each day, to be playing and creating as artists do. For many years I was miserable with my inability to couple my nature as an artist with my career as an Educator. I resented going to work when all I wanted to do was write. I was looking at the hours in my day as an impediment, rather than an opportunity, and I needed only to notice what life was showing me. Those hours weren't only a measure of the time that I had on any given day, those hours were a measure of how I was experiencing my life day in and day out. Viewing time as a measure of experience changed everything for me. When the opportunity arose, I decided to take a new assignment within the school system that allowed for more play and creativity. My new role not only filled my days with more joy, but drastically reduced the amount of time I was spending on unnecessary paperwork and emails. In turn, this created more space in my life for writing. All I needed was to shift the way that I was thinking about time, and to turn those hours of my day into the best experience possible. We can be creative in the way that we define and measure time, even with limitations. Losing an income stream to live our dream life is a major limitation for most. So what is a possible solution? First, ask yourself **What does my dream life look like?** List everything that you envision. Big things, like what you will be doing and where you will be living; and little things, like what you can feel, hear, or smell. Once you've taken enough time to do this, ask yourself **Which parts of my dream life do I already have?** Using my own dream life as an example, it's clear to see from the chart below that I was already living out parts of my dream when my colleague had asked that question, I just hadn't realized it yet. Once I contemplated what I already had in life, I could see that I would always be a writer no matter where I was in this world, that I was well traveled as it were, and that I could hear the tinkling echoes of windchimes in my backyard whenever I wanted to.

What I Had	What I Dreamed Of Having
Work /debt	Financial freedom /flexibility
10 min drive to the lake	Living on the ocean
Writing	Writing
Travel	Travel
The sound of chimes	The sound of chimes

Not exactly the dream life, but I became filled with excitement when realizing what I already had, because it meant that I was already *in* my dream life. It wasn't *out there somewhere*, it was merely incomplete. I could begin to find ways to bring more peace into my life or connect with more writers. I could focus on paying down my debt and possibly even move. I knew at that moment that I would take control of my life, that I would not be blown off course by circumstance, and that everything I did from that point onward would be done in the pursuit of my dream. True self-mastery tells us that our dream life is and always has been in motion. It isn't a future life outside of us, and so, what matters is how we turn up in it each day. We can know what it looks like, and can see where we are along the way, but what we're really trying to master each day is bringing together and keeping under control the things that we value most in life. It could be our work, our relationships, our fitness level, or all of these combined. It doesn't matter what it is, only that every day we have the opportunity to master it. In time, you may come to see that losing an income stream to pursue a dream life wasn't the problem that needed addressing after all; it isn't a lack of money or opportunity preventing us from experiencing the life that we want, it isn't even our greatest fear. After discovering in ourselves what it is that we desire, after finding our courage and mastering our state of mind, the one thing that can thwart everything is how effectively we are able to master our day. Mastering our day means never letting anyone or anything else be in control of it, never working towards someone else's dream, and never putting time towards things that don't matter. To truly transform and master ourselves, we establish those things that we value most, and we place them in the center of everything. There is no one-size-fits-all way of doing this. Everyone has unique lives and circumstances that require different daily routines. The invitation here is that you give some thought to how enjoyable your daily life is, and what you could change to make it better. My daily schedule is based on the four things I value most in life; *my health & well-being*, *my family*, *my work*, and *my craft*. Rather than viewing my day hour by hour, I view it as three distinct phases of my circadian rhythm. Each phase works in tandem with what my mind and body naturally want to do, so nothing feels forced as it once did. Each day I'm fulfilling those things that I value most, and when I feel like I'm mastering this, everything flows beautifully. Stressful events will always occur, but my schedule is designed in such a way that it acts as a buffer. When there are too many external things pulling me away from what's important, or I begin to feel out of control, I can easily identify which phase is being impacted, and the things that I need to do more or less of.

Phase 1 5:00 am - 1:00 pm	Phase 2 1:00 pm - 9:00 pm	Phase 3 9:00 pm - 5:00 am
Watch sunrise	Teach /write	Connect w/ family
Exercise	Connect w/ family	Write /read
Eat first meal	Pamper self	Meditate
Teach	Watch sunset	Sleep

When your daily schedule aligns with what you value most, and when you are staying consistent in your daily practices and working towards a life that you dream of, you are mastering yourself and your experience of life. There will be times when dinner escapes you, or when you just can't do that morning walk. Seek to understand the reasons why and resolve to avoid the same from happening tomorrow. In this way, you remain the master of your day. It's only when we become victims of circumstance, pulled in every direction by people, things, and chaos, that we become masters of nothing. Do not give up after one bad day, but instead, ask yourself why you had it and work towards a solution. Do not strive for perfection; forgive yourself easily and allow for change when change is necessary. We are designed to be in flux, constantly progressing and learning new things. Create an environment that is going to support that positively. Be selective about who and what you're listening to. Not only in the shows you might watch, or the material you might read, but in your friends and family. When we surround ourselves with small-minded people who want to argue or waste time, it becomes difficult to expand. It's like walking into a room full of smokers, you won't be able to breathe. When we surround ourselves with open-minded people who want to grow and evolve, it becomes easy to explore our curiosities. It's like walking into a room full of musicians, you can't help but to tap your toes. There will always be people offering advice or viewpoints, and you have the power to sift through these voices. Especially listen to the people who are lifting you, celebrating your wins, and motivating you. Here in the thermosphere, you are establishing your **new home base**; a default way of interacting with the world as the highest version of you. Do not take for granted how easy it is to cradle yourself back into the arms of fear and comfort, back into the habits so familiar to you -habits that rob you of the opportunity to live joyfully and free. If something is draining you, find a way to change it or rid yourself of it; if something is bringing you happiness or ease, find a way to keep it in your life regularly. Although it might not feel like the dream life just yet, this is your all-star path towards it. Life is meant to be enjoyed, friend, not in some distant moment in the future, but right now. You may be inclined to believe that there is some final destination; a journey's end that will bring you everything you've ever desired. The truth is, if there was such a place with nothing left to explore or attain, you might drift about aimlessly -if not go mad. Self-mastery is not a final destination. It is our never-ending pursuit of improvement and the refinement of our very existence. That's what gives us joy. I feel joy in this moment as I write this book, unpublished and unread by anyone. And wasn't that always the way for you? Think of when you made it on a team or landed a job interview. Every time you've felt progress in your life, chances are you have felt joy. We think it's from the reward of making a team or landing a job, but real joy comes from our understanding of the toil that came before it; the actions that were taken each day to achieve what we wanted. Nietzsche insisted that we should learn from artists how to make things beautiful, attractive, and desirable for ourselves when they are not. He spoke about the artistic method of stepping back from something until there are plenty of things one can no longer see, and in many ways, our lives can be viewed in the same way. When we are improving ourselves we are removing and reworking the less desirable parts to create something more beautiful, to self-fashion ourselves into anything our hearts desire. What does it mean to become an exceptional person, parent, or friend? Each step or change towards the style that you want to give to your life and character is a step in the right direction. Your life is your masterpiece, and in it are your days. You are the master sculptor, carving and shaping your most beautiful life, removing waste and smoothing its edges. Not for that one day that you can stand back and say, *"Yes, this is a masterpiece,"* but for the joy that can be found in the present moment each day, carving, shaping, and smoothing.

Evoke Your Highest Self

Chapter Companion

In the previous chapter, *Self-Mastery*, I went through the process of how to recognize the degree to which one feels a sense of alignment with their true purpose in life; how much control they have over their daily routine, and how to change their circumstances when something doesn't feel right. Reevaluating our relationship with time, and using what we value most in life as an anchor to our daily schedules, are two powerful and tangible tools that I discussed in this chapter. Before applying these same tools to your own life, spend some time reflecting on the questions outlined in the Face 4 Quiz on the pages that follow. Get honest about how you feel when thinking about your relationship, job, health, and home. Next, using the Dream Life Chart, put to paper the kind of life you secretly long for, and compare it with what you already have in life. Try to discover how far along you already are in your dream life, as opposed to how far away it may seem to you. Even this small shift in thinking can dramatically impact how you feel each day, and the perspective that you have on your life. Finally, play around with the Daily Schedule Chart to determine what needs to be done to get you closer to what you desire, even if it means trying several different ways of doing things until finding a flow that works for you. Ideally, each part of your day will align with what is most important to you and will eliminate anything that isn't. Spend time thinking about how much you value time with family, time alone, exercising, working, or creating. To help in this process, a list of some common values can be found in the section entitled 'What's Important To You'. Give yourself full permission to get excited about designing your life in this way, about developing a routine that you know deep inside will be less stressful for you and the people you care about, and will bring more fulfilment to your life and to theirs.

The Face 4 Quiz

The Face-4 Quiz asks you to face 4 big areas of your life and rate them on a scale of 1 to 5 (see below for a description of each rating). The effectiveness of the quiz will depend on how much reflection, humility, and honesty you give to it. For each question, circle a number between 1 and 5. Then tally and reflect on your total score.

1 - Unbearable; I feel miserable in this area of my life and cant take it
2 - Frustrated; I feel like something has to give in this area of my life
3 - Neutral; I feel neither terrible or fantastic in this area of my life
4 - Content; I feel satisfied with this area of my life, even if it's not perfect
5 - Awesome; I feel like this area of my life has no trouble spots at all

How do I feel about my marriage/relationship/single life?

1   2   3   4   5

How do I feel about my job/career/level of education?

1   2   3   4   5

How do I feel about my overall health?

1   2   3   4   5

How do I feel about my home/where I live?

1   2   3   4   5

Calculate your total score. Evaluate how much you agree or disagree with its corresponding statement.

4-8 Points: There may be several areas of your life that are negatively impacting your mental, physical, and spiritual health. There may be an urgent need for change. You could seek a professional.

9-12 Points: You may be feeling tired, overwhelmed, or stuck in your current circumstances. You may want to make changes but aren't sure how. You could engage in self-directed learning.

13-16 Points: There may be one or more areas of your life that motivate you, but something could be leaving you with a sense of boredom. You could create changes in this specific area of your life.

17-20 Points: You may enjoy a change in one or more areas of your life, or you may need to dig a little deeper with your answers. You could explore whether there is a need for change.

Dream Life Chart

Start by listing the most important things you dream of having, and then list what you have already. Think about several areas of your life, both tangible (things you can see and touch, such as a home) and non-tangible (things you can feel, such as love or respect).

What I Have	What I Dream Of Having

Daily Schedule Chart

List what is important for you to accomplish in each phase of your day. Be thoughtful in this process; some things are fixed, such as work, and some are fluid, such as hobbies. Remember that you have the power to make changes if something is not aligning with what you value most. Adjust times as needed.

What's Important to you?

As you begin to think about how you can schedule your time in a way that aligns with what you value, take a moment to reflect on the list below. Circle the words that stand out for you, and then see how you can incorporate them into your schedule.

Family	Friendship	Growth	Nature
Fitness	Community	Success	Solitude
Nutrition	Leisure	Teamwork	Beauty
Spirituality	Creativity	Contribution	Adventure
Self-Care	Play	Wealth	Freedom

Phase 1 Time Window ___-___	**Phase 2** Time Window ___-___	**Phase 3** Time window ___-___

Joy & Freedom
Life in the Exosphere

"If I love myself, I love you. If I love you, I love myself" Rumi

I learned a simple yet powerful lesson as a young girl while observing my mother in the garden one day. I remember watching intently as she carefully removed a plant from its container and placed it into a second container much larger in size. I couldn't see anything wrong with the first container, so I asked my mother why she was moving the plant. She explained to me that no matter how much she was fertilizing and watering the plant, it wasn't going to grow as big as it could; the roots would expand and reach outwards until they touched the sides of the container, sending a message to the plant to stop growing. My mother needed to move the plant so that it could grow to its full potential; a lesson that has stuck with me for life. Any time that I begin to feel the limitations of my reach, I too, seek a bigger container to grow in, and now that container has become the entire world around me. I often wonder if, on some divine level, I knew exactly what to do to push good fortune and health away from me, causing the more difficult events in my life. I grew so much during those times and felt immense joy once reaching the other side of them. We think we may understand the world around us, why things happen, and who or what the driving forces are; we look outwards to solve this puzzle when all along it is us at the helm of our destinies. When we deny ourselves our power to transform -our ability to create joy in ourselves and others -we are taking an incomplete journey, like the plant that fails to grow. When we utilise our power to transform we not only flourish in the external world, we expand our hearts beyond their known boundaries to find peace and coherence deep inside of ourselves. That is freedom, the freedom we were born with, and it can never be taken away.

To know the beauty of living in the exosphere is to know the beauty in all of life. It is synonymous with experiences of joy and freedom, and perhaps the greatest kind of clarity we can open ourselves up to receiving. One of the greatest misconceptions, however, is that experiences of joy and freedom are something that happens at the end of one's journey, like a beautiful moment that marks the end of all suffering. Looking at joy and freedom from the perspective of *when it happens,* doesn't leave much room for the more rewarding perspective of *how it happens*. I have felt myself in an exospheric state on more than one occasion. I have felt it in some remarkable moments, like when standing in the sand on a long Californian beach, and I have felt it in less remarkable moments, like when sitting at a table inside of a noisy restaurant. Each time, I felt as if I were floating above myself, seeing everything around me from the highest vantage point. I could see my body and the immediate space that I was in, including the people around me, and I could see outside of that, including the buildings and wide open spaces. One time in particular I truly felt as if I had somehow jutted myself through each layer of the atmosphere, and was now drifting blissfully in space. Yet, there I was, standing in my kitchen, listening to my estranged husband talk. Nothing he could say would penetrate my mind or have any effect on my emotion. I had come to love myself again, and was embarking on a new chapter in my life. I was mastering myself in new ways, and truly understood that I could take myself out of this circumstance with him; this body; this kitchen; this house; this street; this city; this country; this world; until all that was left was a being, looking down on what human life I had created for myself; the suffering I felt and allowed myself to feel with another human, the stress I felt about whether or not I could pay my bills after Christmas, the weight I felt in my body after not taking proper care of it, and all of the *things* piling up as I looked around my house. Emotionally detached from it all, I marveled at how many trinkets I would keep over the years, mementos of memories that I was holding on to as if living them were lost. Over the next several months, I filled over a dozen boxes with nick-nacks, housewares, and clothing. Anything I didn't want or need was boxed up and placed in the back of my car to be delivered to a donation dropoff site. I sifted through each room of my house like an internal excavation. I carved my bedroom closet down to essentials and joyful accessories only; I carefully selected only the best products that I owned for my ensuite washroom; I rid myself of *extra* sheets and towels from the linen closet; *extra* ladles and jar openers from the kitchen; and I rummaged through photographs in the basement, reflecting on how often we struggle at the foot of our own importance -as if our story, our life, our photographs, and grand human voyage is all that there is. I basked in this new level of consciousness, with my life stripped down to its minimal parts, and the feeling of weightlessness I had always yearned for. I managed to sell a few thousand dollars worth of what little equity I had, and although I didn't have much, I had this feeling inside of me that felt priceless. People would talk and all I would hear were stories; their stories, my stories, all the stories of the world; like the low rumbling of life's belly in an all-encompassing hum. I went out dancing for the first time in years and felt a sense of unity and compassion for all strangers. There was a new kind of love in my heart, and I wanted people to know that I loved them in the way that I now loved myself. I wanted to share my experiences with people, in hopes that they would see themselves too. I would go into coffee shops and strike up conversations, and I would look into the eyes of everyone I met. I would see their pain, sometimes feeling it like my own, and I would take the time to listen to them without judgment. By getting outside of myself, the clarity I received was how important it was for me to simply love and to give to other humans. I saw the compounding effect of this, and I understood, all at once, how deeply connected we all are. *The power of the universe; the power of you; the power of others.* During this time, I was driving home from work one day when I came to an intersection and waited for the light to turn green. The sky held the early warning signs of Winter, when snowflakes fall slow enough for their outlines to be seen, and as more and more snowflakes fell onto my windshield, I stared blankly across the road at the driver opposite me. He appeared to be in his late seventies and was staring and waiting as blankly as I was. *I wonder what that man did with his life*, I thought. *I wonder what I will do with mine.* While sheer curtains of snow fell between us, I could still see some detail in his worn face, and in that moment I felt immense love for that man. That period in my life felt as though I had opened a door to the expanse of the universe and it was pouring into me alone. Everything was working like a well-oiled machine. I had perspective, integrity, energy, and harmony. I felt aligned, accomplished, and certain that this is what it meant to feel joyous and free. But it was what happened next, suddenly and inexplicably, that taught me the greatest lesson of all. From this apex of consciousness that I had reached within myself, I started to nosedive, without warning, into a deep internal spiral. Over the next several weeks, I could feel myself plummeting towards darkness, consumed by emotion, familiar cravings, and the temptation to fall back on old habits and patterns. I struggled with my demons in a state of confused introspection, wondering if joy or freedom were sustainable at all, until one day I could finally see it. I had fallen back mentally, but I hadn't fallen back to my place of comfort and protection in the home base I had always known. Had I crashed down to the troposphere of life again, I would be looking upwards for the answers and downwards in despair. But I was not looking upwards or downwards this time. I was looking around, looking at myself, and I could see that I was in my place of learning, honing, and building. I was in the thermosphere of life, where I had already learned to master myself in so many ways. But why did I fall at all? I always imagined that once I had experienced joy and freedom in my life I would feel it forever; and while it's true that I had reached incredible heights within myself, I quickly learned that a destination was not what I was ever seeking. Every time we reach a new peak within ourselves, that growth urges us to spread out even more, like the roots of my mother's plant. We don't put a bulb in the ground and expect a flower to immediately rise from the soil; nor do rocks become sand in a day. A pot of water won't boil until a sufficient measure of time has passed, and like all mammals, we were not born from our mothers without a harrowing struggle for life. We may attempt to remain in the exosphere, but to no effect; we will continue to be a bulb, a rock, cold water, a fetus, you see? We will burn out at the place where we left off because to remain would be to go against nature. We are forced back down to the thermosphere, to learn more, grow more, and practice new acts of courage in unknown territories, so we can return to the exosphere and share what we've learned with others. When that happens, an even deeper sense of joy and freedom can be felt, until, whether by boredom or some newfound inspiration, stressors or exhaustion, we inevitably seek change in our lives to challenge or transform ourselves once again.

We can often sense a transformation happening in our lives by the way that we become disrupted in them. When I found myself reverting backwards, it was a disruption to my life and happiness. I didn't realize it in the moment, but in hindsight I had taken myself as far as I could in my growth, and it was my lack of motivation that disrupted my sense of peace, while leading me to search for a deeper understanding of myself at the same time. We can become disrupted in many different ways, including our health, our work, and our family life. When we can see and understand our disruptions, we can appreciate how it is that they help us, like the plant roots feeling for their limitations before sending a stop signal. For instance, if we are bored with our work, then what we are doing could lack purpose or meaning. A disruption reminds us of this. Even if we feel like we're regressing, we may just be needing a change. Sometimes we are so tired and overwhelmed by our day-to-day lives that an escape or distraction can be found through our sabotage. It can be exciting to lose ourselves in a crunchy snack, or comforting to sleep in that extra hour. The required, sustained, and repetitive effort that goes toward our pursuits can lead us down the path of self-destruction. By their very nature we grow tired of our own goals, not because they don't matter to us anymore, but because we are ready to master something greater. Instead of responding to a disruption in a low state, however, we can bring in the high state habits that we've already mastered into new endeavors. It struck me that I would never reach a place in my life where I would feel a sense of completion. I would always be somewhere in its cyclical nature, but it didn't have to be sinister, it could be joyous instead. I had reached a space where I wasn't aiming for balance blindly anymore. I grew to understand my stop signals, what was happening inside of me, and I had complete control over what I would do next. We don't need to damage ourselves with poor sleep or diet simply because we've become bored or stressed; we can take walks and hot showers, or we can dream about new endeavors. Learning the art of this exceptional way to live, not crashing and burning back to our beginnings, but floating effortlessly between these two atmospheres, is the best view of life that I have come to know. It is from this space, where we are constantly refining ourselves, growing and expanding, that we can experience all of life's joy and freedom. It is from this space that we can tap into our greatest selves and serve others wholeheartedly, where we not only discover the gift in ourselves, but we become a gift to the people around us.

Life is a celebration each day -one that we show up to in our best outfit, with our best smile, and with our best intentions. When we live as if life is a celebration we naturally want to give gifts every day. The gifts can be big or small, and they can be tangible or intangible. We thrive off of the joy of giving them because we are doing exactly what the universe wants us to do, and it gives us purpose and meaning. Spreading joy to others is the ultimate dream no matter what your dreams are. This book has been an act of love, baring my soul and stripping these thoughts and feelings naked, so that you may read them in the most honest way. This is our life force; continuous progress and growth despite the unknown. The more we love, the more we give, and the more we give, the more we expand. What more do you believe we are here for, if not to love and be loved; if not to feed and be fed; if not to create and grow like the creeping thyme of a cosmic garden? You do not have to struggle to find meaning and purpose in your life; you were born with meaning and designed with a purpose. Instead, find ways to grow and contribute, to expand your sense of joy and freedom. Find an adventure, and allow an adventure to find *you*; you will understand your purpose in all of it. Along the way, you will fall and struggle, and that is part of all its beauty. Eventually, after many falls and struggles, you will learn to fall less often, recover quickly, and surround yourself with people, moments, and memories. You will learn to live in a way that, if you were to live it over, you wouldn't change a thing. That is the sport of it -the end game -and why we do what we do to improve. We want our lives to resemble the crisp lines of a neatly folded shirt or the timed collapse of a thousand waves. Over and over, we try to get this right; we try to match the beauty and grandeur of life itself, feeling for its rhythm in our cacophony and failing miserably time and again. Keep going. Notice the moments when your exertion pays off, or when others express gratitude for your friendship or support. Notice the inexplicable moments of grace in your life and how you feel when you can't quite explain why something turns out the way that it does, or where you suddenly see perfection and feel peace in a outcome. It isn't an unreachable space or something we may only experience once in our lifetime if we're lucky. It is a space that's been waiting for us since the moment we were born. It is our ultimate pilgrimage and a space we can be in many times over in our lifetime. When we experience joy and freedom through our childlike desire to create and to give, we can do the things we feel compelled to do with our lives, and then share those gifts and lessons with others. That's all any of us are doing, isn't it? Whether it's the billionaire on his boat or a single mother who's writing a book, the guru who's best friends with Oprah or the college graduate starting his own business, we're all just exploring and playing as we once did as children, aren't we? When we grow weary or restless we can simply move on and learn something new. We can continue to learn, create, and contribute; and by doing this, we might just find the meaning of it all.

Navigate Your Life

Chapter Companion

In the final chapter, *Joy and Freedom*, I explained that it is us at the helm of our own destinies; that by using our own power to transform, create and contribute, we sustain joy in ourselves and towards others. This is how we come to find peace and coherence in our lives, and in our long journey for freedom. I explained in the chapter how I came to recognize my own vicious cycle as a friendly reminder that it is time to learn something new or to hone learned skills that we may have forgotten. This reminder, however, doesn't always come to us in a way that appears friendly, and often feels like a disruption to our lives; poor eating; overspending; news binging; infidelity; conflict; health issues; a disorderly home; or trouble at work. It's an unsettledness we may feel, a block in our hearts, and an endless invasion of thoughts in our heads. When this happens, it's important to remember that you have a choice about how to respond. Over the years, my list of high-state habits came about quite organically, and was eventually imparted to my family and loved ones. It seems fitting to share the list here, and I hope it serves as a gentle reminder when you may need it most, or perhaps inspire you to create your own list. Display the list (or your own variation of it) somewhere that you will be able to view daily.

We get outside and move our bodies;
We don't watch the news or tabloids

We cook wholesome meals;
We don't *drive through* anything anymore

We pamper ourselves intentionally;
We don't harm ourselves mindlessly

We join a class or community;
We don't sit and scroll through people online

We create something that moves us;
We don't focus on what we're missing

We write down our thoughts;
We don't argue bitterly, or bottle up feelings

We absorb a new book or podcast;
We don't know all that there is to know

We help others, and we love with our hearts;
We know we are one of many

We organize our life and home;
We don't let the world pile up around us

Reflect on three of your own low-state habits (things you do that are self-sabotaging, but soothing at times) and write each one beside the words "I don't." Beside the words "I," reflect on three high-state habits (things you do that are good *for* you) that you could do instead. Once finished, read your list out loud. If you aren't sure where to begin, simply choose what resonates with you most from the list provided on the opposite page.

My High State Habits

I _____

I don't_____

I _____

I don't_____

I _____

I don't_____

Writing down your high-state habits helps you to navigate your way through your own life disruptions in two different ways.

On one hand, having a visual cue in plain view will ensure that you remember your alternative choices, and on the other hand, when you write something down on a piece of paper, the biological process of encoding occurs in your brain, which reinforces and integrates this into your life even more.

Nearing the end of this chapter I suggested that the meaning of life isn't so complex; we do the things we feel compelled to do in our lives, what we're drawn to, and then we share those gifts and lessons with others. Have you ever noticed that when you're doing something you love, it's as if time has sped up? And when you're doing something you don't love, it's as if time has slowed enough to suck the life out of you? That isn't how you were designed. You were designed to search and explore, to create and to love, and time…well, that's really just a sensation. It can be filled with joy and freedom, or it can be filled with pain and suffering. You didn't think about this as a child. You got on your bike and rode down the street to your friend's house; you spent a little extra time looking at that toy you were saving up for; and you spent hours trying to figure things out, like how to build or fix something broken. You wondered, seemingly forever, how you could become something -and here you are -maybe seeing that there was nothing for you to ever become, because you were everything you ever needed to be from the moment you were born. The list at the end of this chapter, *Over 75 Ways To Discover Joy*, was created to help you to realize both the grand and trivial pursuits that can be joyful; to help you find multiple ways of experiencing a sense of meaning in your life. Not everything on the list will speak directly to you, and some things may be out of your comfort zone. Still, try to pursue as many as you can, and observe how you feel over time. What are you drawn to? What do you feel compelled to do? What would you like to learn or share with others? The answers are not with me or this book; they are inside of you, waiting to be remembered.

Over 75 Ways To Discover Joy

- Hike in a forest
- Climb a mountain
- Sit by the ocean
- Stargaze at night
- Collect rocks, shells
- Stand in the rain
- Plant a garden
- Drive along fields
- Watch the sun rise
- Watch the sun set
- Nurture house plants
- Go whale watching
- Save the whales

- Snuggle with a pet
- Converse with elders
- Meet with friends
- Play with a child
- Go on a date
- Thank an old teacher
- Help a stranger
- Donate to a charity
- Give gifts to people
- Hug someone
- Make eye contact
- Say thank you
- Compliment people

- Volunteer
- Plan a party or event
- Make people laugh
- Bake for loved ones
- Light some candles
- Listen to music
- Have a bubble bath
- Read books
- Meditate daily
- Journal often
- Keep crystals & gems
- Arrange flowers
- Sing

- Go on a road trip
- Camp under the moon
- Visit a museum
- Go to a concert
- Watch live sports
- Watch live comedy
- Drink California Cabs
- Take a train ride
- Traverse old ruins
- Find abandoned things
- Build your own fire
- Restore furniture
- Finish a puzzle

- Play cards & games
- Learn a language
- Make candles
- Paint something
- Learn an instrument
- Take photographs
- Work with clay
- Construct something
- Take a cooking class
- Roast marshmallows
- Sit on a sunny patio
- Visit an Irish pub
- Drink good coffee

- Train for a marathon
- Take cold plunges
- Practice yoga
- Kayak on a lake
- Go for a bike ride
- Dance a lot
- Keep stationary
- Hang chimes
- Grow vegetables
- Curate albums
- Spin a globe
- Fall in love
- Fall in love again

Bibliography

I. Nietzsche, F. W., Geuss, R., Nehamas, A., & Löb, L. (2009). *Friedrich Nietzsche: Writings from the early notebooks.* Cambridge University Press.

II. McCraty, R. (2003). *The Energetic Heart: Bioelectromagnetic Interactions Within and Between People.* Institute of HeartMath.

III. Backster, C. (2003). *Primary Perception: Biocommunication with plants, living foods, and human cells.* White rose millennium Press.

IV. Koob, A. (2009). *The root of thought: Unlocking glia - the brain cell that will help us sharpen our wits, heal injury, and treat brain disease.* FT Press.

V. Tipping, C. C. (2009). *Radical forgiveness: A revolutionary five-stage process to: Heal relationships, let go of anger and blame, and find peace in any situation.* Sounds True.

VI. Benedict, M.-T. (2009). *Journey Through the Light and Back.* Purple Haze Press.

VII. Gottfried, S. (2022). *Women, food, and hormones.* Harvest, an imprint of William Morrow.

VIII. Burgin, T. (2014) *Eight Essential Yoga Lessons for Beginners.* Adhimukti Press.

IX. Te Kulve, Marije, et al. "Early Evening Light Mitigates Sleep Compromising Physiological and Alerting Responses to Subsequent Late Evening Light." *Scientific Reports*, vol. 9, no. 1, 5 Nov. 2019, https://doi.org/10.1038/s41598-019-52352-w.

X. Wehrens, Sophie M.T., et al. "Meal Timing Regulates the Human Circadian System." *Current Biology*, vol. 27, no. 12, 1 June 2017, https://doi.org/10.1016/j.cub.2017.04.059.

About The Author

Katie Miller is a teacher, life strategist, and writer who has dedicated her life to helping both children and adults live healthier, happier, and more serene lives. In addition to her professional membership with the Ontario College of Teachers, she received her formal training in Strategic Intervention at Robbins-Madanes Training under the guidance of Tony Robbins, Cloe Madanes, Mark Peysha, and Magali Peysha. She currently resides with her husband and daughters in the greater Toronto area of Ontario, Canada.

www.ingramcontent.com/pod-product-compliance
Lightning Source LLC
Chambersburg PA
CBHW051559010526
44118CB00023B/2757